Irish Genealogy Without Certainty

When Records Are Missing, Method Matters

Laura Woodward

CAVAN
COUSINS
Press

Library of Congress Control Number: 2026903627

ISBN: 979-8-9947927-1-1

First edition: 2026
Cavan Cousins Press
Royal Oak, Michigan

Use of AI assistance: Portions of this book were drafted and refined with the assistance of AI-based language tools. These tools were used to support organization, clarity, and revision, and were not used as sources of research or authority. All methodological decisions, interpretations of evidence, and conclusions reflect the author's independent judgment and responsibility.

Cover design by Laura Woodward

For permissions requests, contact: cavancousins@gmail.com
Printed in the United States of America

For those who worked carefully
when the records did not cooperate.

How To Use This Book

This book is not intended to be read as a set of instructions or a sequence of steps to be followed mechanically. It is a book about method- about how to think clearly, proportionally, and responsibly when the records are incomplete, ambiguous, or resistant to certainty.

Some chapters build on concepts introduced earlier, particularly those concerned with question design, place-based analysis, and the evaluation of evidence. Readers new to Irish genealogy, or to research in contexts of record loss and migration, may benefit from reading the book in order. More experienced researchers may choose to move between chapters as needed, returning to frameworks and examples as their questions evolve.

The frameworks introduced in this book, SCALE, PLACE, and CLEAR, are not checklists and are not meant to produce answers on their own. They are schematic tools designed to support judgment, not replace it. Their purpose is to help structure questions, constrain interpretation, and make uncertainty visible, rather than to resolve it prematurely.

Examples and diagrams are illustrative rather than determinative. They demonstrate how a method can be applied in practice, not what conclusions should be drawn in other cases. Throughout the book, attention is given not only to what the records suggest, but also to what they cannot support. Readers are encouraged to adapt these approaches to their own research contexts, while remaining attentive to the limits of the evidence available to them.

This book can be used alongside active research. Many readers may find it most useful when read slowly, in parallel with their own projects, returning to particular chapters as new questions arise or as earlier assumptions require revision. The goal is not efficiency, but clarity; not closure, but proportion.

If you remember one thing while reading, let it be this: careful method is not a barrier to discovery. It is the condition that makes discovery meaningful.

Preface

What This Book Is, and Is Not

This book is written for Irish genealogical research as it actually exists, not as we wish it did. It is for researchers working in a record environment shaped by loss, uneven survival, and documents that were never designed to answer modern genealogical questions.

If you've been hoping this book would finally give you clean answers, it's okay to feel disappointed here. Many careful researchers reach that hope only after years of real effort. What this book offers instead is a way to keep working without blaming yourself for what the records can't provide.

This book is a guide to method. Recent scholarship treats genealogy not simply as a personal or narrative pursuit, but as a structured regime of evidence operating across legal, institutional, and historical contexts. Writing in Genealogy, Ayeni (2025) shows how genealogical claims are evaluated in settings such as law, citizenship, and recognition-not through absolute certainty, but through the weighing of multiple forms of evidence, including documents, genetics, and association. In these contexts, transparency about evidentiary limits is not a weakness but a requirement.

Irish genealogy operates within the same logic. Conclusions gain strength not by claiming finality, but by making their foundations, scope, and constraints visible. This approach teaches how to frame questions the records can reasonably answer; how to anchor people to place before assigning identity; how to work with indirect evidence, repeated association, and documented absence; and how to form conclusions that are clearly labeled, proportionate to the evidence, and open to revision.

This book is not a promise of certainty. It is also not a promise of resolution for every line. It is a promise of clarity, restraint, and conclusions that can be shared without apology.

It does not offer shortcuts, miracle tools, or techniques for forcing answers where the evidence does not support them. It does not equate restraint with paralysis. Working without definitive proof does not mean stopping; it means moving forward responsibly. Hypotheses are tools, not guesses. Trees are workspaces, not verdicts. Conclusions are strongest when their limits are visible.

Above all, this book is grounded in respect: for the records that survived, for the people whose lives are being reconstructed, and for fellow researchers who will inherit what we publish and share.

When certainty is unavailable, the work is not to stop, but to proceed in ways that remain honest, flexible, and worthy of trust.

Table Of Contents

Unit I: Thinking Clearly Before You Search

Irish genealogy doesn't start with records. It starts with thinking. This unit gives you a repeatable way to think so your searches produce structure instead of sprawl.

If this feels slower than the way you're used to researching, that's intentional. Slowing down at this stage prevents years of cleanup later.

Method, mindset, and ethical restraint.

Pausing before you search can feel wrong because modern genealogy tools reward motion, not reflection. Hints and automated suggestions keep you clicking. When results don't clarify anything, the default response is to search wider or switch platforms instead of checking the assumptions driving the search.

This unit is a deliberate pause: not as a mood, but as a method.

Irish genealogy is a record-limited research environment. That means conclusions have to be proportional to what the sources were created to capture and what has survived (Bloch, 1953; Braudel, 1980).

The goal is not to lower standards. It is to apply standards that fit the evidence: careful source evaluation, transparent reasoning, and conclusions stated only as strongly as the records support.

This method keeps work accurate, flexible, and shareable even when definitive identity chains are not possible.

Chapter 1: You're Not Stuck- The Question Is Too Big

Most people come to Irish genealogy already worn down. They've searched widely, subscribed to multiple databases, tested DNA, contacted distant matches, and followed every promising hint. This isn't casual research. It's persistent, serious effort. And yet one line refuses to move.

A familiar stall looks like this:

Patrick Reilly

- Born: Ireland
- Married: New York
- Died: Brooklyn
- No parish.
- No townland.

No parents.

Questions like these are common:

- Who were his parents?
- Where exactly in Ireland was she born?
- Which Patrick Reilly is mine?

If this description feels uncomfortably familiar, you're not alone.

Years can pass in this state. New tools appear. Record collections expand. DNA match lists get longer. But nothing changes in substance. Eventually, frustration turns inward. Researchers begin to assume they are missing something obvious or that others possess a skill they somehow lack.

If you've been working hard and still feel stuck, this usually isn't about effort, experience, or intelligence. Most often, it means the question you're asking is bigger than what the surviving records can reasonably answer (Bloch, 1953; Fischer, 1970).

Why Careful Research Still Stalls

Irish genealogy rarely stalls because evidence is completely missing. More often, it stalls because the research question assumes answers the records were never designed to provide.

Questions like these are common:

- Who were his parents?

- Where exactly in Ireland was she born?

- Which Patrick Reilly is mine?

These are reasonable questions. They are also, in many cases, unanswerable at the beginning of Irish research.

Irish records were created for local administrative, religious, and legal purposes. They were not designed to establish modern, multigenerational identity chains. Relationships are often implied rather than stated. Geographic boundaries overlap. Record survival varies sharply by time and place.

When a question asks more than the records can support, research does not move forward. It repeats. The goal here isn't to lower your expectations or stop caring about answers. It's to change the size of the question so the records have a chance to respond.

Scale Before Search

Records only become useful when the question matches what they were created to answer. This principle- scale before search- is foundational in Irish genealogy.

Big questions about who someone was can quietly steer your research in the wrong direction. They encourage early merging of individuals, overconfident interpretation, and selective reading of evidence (Fischer, 1970). Smaller questions grounded in place and time do the opposite. They allow evidence to accumulate, constrain possibilities, and reveal patterns gradually.

This chapter is not about finding new records. It is about aligning your questions with what records can actually support.

Reducing Scope Without Reducing Rigor

Shrinking a question does not mean lowering standards. It means making progress possible. It replaces the exhausting hunt for a single perfect record with a process that builds evidence in layers.

Most stalled research is driven by a single, persistent question. When that question includes words like who, exact, prove, or definitively, it is often too large for the available evidence.

Examples include

- Who were Patrick Reilly's parents?

- Exactly where in Ireland was she born?

- Can DNA prove this line?

These questions aren't wrong. They just belong later, after smaller questions have done their work.

Replacing Identity With Place and Time

Irish genealogy becomes workable when questions are anchored in location and period instead of identity. In Irish research, identity is rarely declared by a single record. It emerges slowly through repetition, constraint, and consistency (Ginzburg, 1989).

Place limits the number of possible individuals. Time narrows overlapping lives. Associations- such as sponsors, witnesses, and neighbors- reveal patterns without naming relationships directly (Bourdieu, 1977; Massey, 1994).

When identity is pursued first, these stabilizing forces are skipped and ambiguity multiplies. When identity is allowed to emerge last, it rests on structure instead of assumption.

More productive questions often sound like this:

- Which parish served this townland in the 1850s?

- Which Patrick Reilly appears consistently in one location over time?

- Which records place this family in the same area repeatedly?

These questions are less dramatic, but they work. They create boundaries, reduce noise, and let patterns form.

If You Remember One Thing

Feeling stuck usually means the question is too big for the records, not that the research has failed.

One way to remember this is SCALE:

- **S**ize the question you're asking
- **C**heck what the records were built to answer
- **A**sk smaller questions first, grounded in place and time
- **L**et patterns form before drawing conclusions
- **E**xpand the question only when the evidence supports it

When research stalls, revisiting the scale of the question often restores movement without adding new tools or sources.

S	Size the question you're asking
C	Check what the records were built to answer
A	Ask smaller questions first, grounded in place and time
L	Let patterns form before drawing conclusions
E	Expand the question only when the evidence supports it

Chapter 2: Scale Before Search, Asking Questions Records Can Answer

Once researchers accept that they are not stuck because of personal limitation, a quieter problem often appears. The mindset has shifted, but the process has not. Searching continues much as before, just with renewed determination. Broad date ranges are entered. Entire counties are searched at once. Multiple record types are consulted in parallel.

The results feel scattered, contradictory, or inconclusive, and confidence stays low.

This often happens when the research question and the evidence are still misaligned. Even a thoughtful question will fail if it assumes records can answer things they were never meant to capture. Before any record becomes useful, the question guiding the search has to match the purpose of that record.

Here, the focus is on question design: the skill that makes every later search cleaner. Its goal is not to tell you where to search, but to clarify what to ask before you search. When questions are properly scaled, records stop feeling random. Patterns begin to form.

Why Good Questions Still Go Unanswered

It is easy to assume records exist to confirm identity, especially when modern tools present results that way. That assumption is understandable, and it is mostly incompatible with the reality of Irish recordkeeping.

Irish records were not created for future genealogists. They were created to meet immediate administrative, religious, and legal needs (Bloch, 1953). Most were meant to document religious rites, manage land and taxation, record civil events, or track populations. When research questions assume records were meant to establish lineage, reliably separate same-named individuals, or explain family relationships across generations, frustration is almost guaranteed (Fischer, 1970). They were not designed to establish lineage, reliably separate same-named individuals, or explain family relationships across generations.

When research questions assume records were meant to do those things, frustration is almost guaranteed. The problem in these cases is not the researcher and not the record. It can still feel personal when searches don't work. That reaction is human, even when you understand the logic behind it. It lies in the expectation placed on the evidence.This distinction trips up experienced researchers as often as beginners. It's a process issue, not a skill gap.

Goals Are Not Questions

One of the most common sources of confusion in genealogy is mixing up a search goal with a research question. A search goal describes what you ultimately want to know. A research question describes what the evidence can reasonably answer right now.

Identifying Patrick Reilly's parents may be a valid long-term goal. A question like which Patrick Reilly appears consistently in one location before 1865 is far more likely to be answerable with surviving records.

When these two ideas blur, researchers repeat the same searches without gaining clarity. When evidence is pushed to deliver conclusions it can't support, the work often starts to feel exhausting or discouraging- even when you're still putting in real effort.

Good research questions are usually small, tied to a certain time and place, and worth asking- even if you don't end up with a clear answer.

The Problem of Hidden Assumptions

Many stalled questions carry assumptions so familiar they go unnoticed. These assumptions shape how searches are run and how evidence is read, often without any conscious decision.

Common assumptions include believing there was only one person with a given name, assuming records were created where events occurred, assuming parish and civil boundaries align neatly, assuming records survive evenly across regions, or assuming identity was clearer in the past than it is today.

Irish records challenge all of these ideas. When assumptions go unexamined, they quietly limit what you allow the evidence to show- often without you realizing it.

Rewriting Questions to Match Record Purpose

Irish research becomes more productive when questions are shaped by what records reliably contain, not by what we hope they will reveal.

Instead of asking who someone's parents were, a more workable question is which households with a particular surname appear repeatedly in the same townland over time. Instead of asking where someone was born exactly, it is often more useful to ask which parishes appear consistently across a family's records.

These questions rarely produce quick answers. What they produce is structure.

Knowing What Records Can Actually Tell You

Every record type has limits, and sound interpretation depends on knowing those limits.

Church records are generally reliable for establishing presence in a parish, participation in a religious community, and recurring associations through sponsors and witnesses. They rarely support multi-generation proof, clear separation of same-named individuals, or precise birthplaces beyond a parish or chapel.

Land records are strong for placing individuals or families in specific townlands and tracking stability or movement over time. They can suggest proximity to other families and long-term residence. They rarely identify parent-child relationships, give exact ages, or explain why tenancies changed.

When questions go beyond those limits, interpretation becomes speculative rather than analytical.

What This Looks Like in Practice

A researcher finds two baptismal records for children of a man named Patrick Reilly, recorded in different parishes within the same decade. The first impulse is to ask which baptism belongs to the researcher's ancestor.

That framing assumes there is a single correct answer and that it can be identified immediately.

A more useful question is whether these records represent one family using more than one church or two separate families with the same name. That question allows both possibilities to remain open while the researcher maps parishes, compares sponsors, checks land records, and keeps the individuals separate until evidence supports a merge.

Evaluating Whether a Question Fits the Evidence

Before beginning a search, it helps to pause and consider what the record type reliably provides, what it rarely or never provides, and whether the question stays within those bounds.

When it does not, revising the question first often saves time and prevents misinterpretation later.

A Brief Composite Case: The Brennan Problem (Why "Scale Before Search" Works)

A researcher has been working on Mary Brennan, who married in Brooklyn in 1872. The marriage record gives her birthplace as "Ireland" and her age, but not her parents. Over decades, census entries shift between "Ireland" and a more specific county claim that appears only once, late, and secondhand. After years of searching Irish baptisms directly-across multiple sites, indexes, and spellings-nothing resolves.

At this point, the question "Who were Mary Brennan's parents?" feels like the only question that matters. But it is also an identity question that assumes records can do something Irish records often cannot do on demand: name the link that modern researchers want. The records allow a different kind of progress. They allow place- and association-based structure that narrows what is plausible and testable.

So the researcher rescales. Instead of hunting for Mary's baptism as a single missing key, they begin mapping Brennans in land and parish contexts, tracking repeating sponsors and neighbors, and reading Brooklyn records as a system of voices rather than a set of isolated facts. The outcome is not certainty. It is movement: the field narrows from "somewhere in Ireland" to a small, testable set of places and clusters that can be checked against later evidence, including DNA.

The records allow structure; they do not yet allow parentage. That distinction is what keeps stalled research from turning into distorted certainty.

If You Remember One Thing

Records become useful only when the question matches what they were created to answer.

Chapter 3: Evidence-Based Hypotheses and Honest Uncertainty

Once researchers learn to scale their questions and align them with what records can realistically answer, a different kind of stall often appears. At this stage, the issue is no longer a lack of information. Records have been gathered. Patterns are starting to show. A possible connection feels close.

And then the work freezes.

What causes this pause is usually not confusion, but fear. That fear doesn't mean you're reckless or unprepared. It usually means you care deeply about getting this right. Researchers worry about being wrong. They worry about misleading others or damaging their credibility. They worry that moving forward without absolute proof is irresponsible.

In Irish genealogy, responsible work often requires moving forward tentatively. As a result, research can stall again-not because evidence is missing, but because the standard being applied cannot be met.

As you've likely already seen, Irish genealogy rarely produces final proof in the modern sense. Waiting for certainty in this context often means waiting indefinitely. In this chapter, you'll see how to move forward responsibly without pretending certainty exists.

Why Uncertainty Is Not a Personal Failure

Many Irish records never survived. Others were never created. Some document only fragments of the relationships researchers are trying to reconstruct. Parish registers have gaps. Administrative boundaries shift. Names repeat within families and communities. Civil and land records often omit parentage entirely. In smaller populations, endogamy adds another layer of complexity.

In Irish genealogy, waiting for absolute proof often means waiting indefinitely, not because you lack rigor, but because the surviving record rarely names identity in the direct way the question demands.

Responsible research does not require certainty. It requires honesty about what the evidence can and cannot support (Mills, 2017).

When certainty isn't available, aim to stay CLEAR:

- Clearly label assumptions

- Limit conclusions to what the evidence supports

- Explain why a connection is being considered

- Allow room for revision as new information appears

- Respect the limits of the records themselves

CLEAR thinking allows research to move forward while remaining transparent, shareable, and worthy of trust.

C	Clearly label assumptions
L	Limit conclusions to what the evidence supports
E	Explain why a connection is being considered
A	Allow room for revision
R	Respect the limits of the records themselves

If the word hypothesis feels intimidating, it doesn't need to be. Here, it's simply a way to keep moving while staying honest.

What an Evidence-Based Working Assumption Is

An evidence-based working assumption is a tentative conclusion grounded in available evidence, explicitly labeled as tentative, and intentionally held open to revision (Peirce, 1931-1958; Mills, 2017). It is not a guess. It is not a shortcut. It is not a claim dressed up as fact.

A working assumption explains why a connection is being considered and invites testing rather than closure (Peirce, 1931-1958). This approach aligns with current professional standards in genealogy. The Board for Certification of Genealogists' 2025 Application Guide reiterates that responsible conclusions are built through clearly articulated hypotheses, systematic testing, and transparent documentation of uncertainty (Board for Certification of Genealogists [BCG], 2025).

Rather than requiring definitive proof at every stage, these standards emphasize traceable reasoning and explicit openness to revision. In record-limited environments, working assumptions are not provisional shortcuts; they are the mechanism that allows research to proceed without misrepresenting what the evidence can support. Their tentative nature is made visible, both to the researcher and to anyone else who encounters the work.

For example, a working assumption might state that the Patrick Reilly in a specific townland is the same man as the New York immigrant, based on repeated associates, consistent location, and an aligned timeline.

Hypotheses allow research to move forward without sacrificing honesty. They acknowledge uncertainty without letting it stop progress.

Guessing Versus Hypothesizing

The difference between guessing and hypothesizing matters.

A guess fills a gap without support. A working assumption explains an observed pattern and invites testing.

Concluding that someone must be your ancestor because the name matches is a guess. Concluding that someone is a possible ancestor because multiple records align in place, time, and associated names is a working assumption.

The second conclusion does not claim certainty. It shows why the connection is being considered and identifies the evidence that supports it.

How Hypotheses Form in Irish Research

In Irish genealogy, hypotheses usually take shape when several strands of evidence begin to line up.

A name appears repeatedly in the same townland or parish. The same witnesses or sponsors recur across church records. Land, church, and civil records show continuity rather than contradiction. No evidence appears that clearly rules the connection out.

DNA evidence, when available, may support the paper trail without defining it.

No single piece establishes the relationship. Taken together, these elements justify a working explanation that can be tested and refined.

What This Looks Like in Practice

A man named Patrick Reilly appears in mid-nineteenth-century land records in a specific townland. Baptism records from the same parish show Patrick Reilly acting repeatedly as a sponsor. A later New York marriage record names a Patrick Reilly whose reported age aligns with the man in Ireland.

No document states parentage or migration.

A rushed approach merges these records immediately and moves on. An evidence-based working assumption states that, based on consistent location, recurring associations, and aligned timelines, this Patrick Reilly is a likely candidate for the New York immigrant, while clearly noting that the conclusion is tentative and subject to revision if conflicting evidence appears.

That framing allows research to continue with focus. It supports targeted searching, careful evaluation of DNA matches connected to the same area, and openness to correction without freezing progress.

Why Clear Labeling Matters

The strength of a working assumption depends on how clearly it is labeled. Clear labeling protects the researcher, keeps shared work from being misunderstood, and protects the people behind the records (Board for Certification of Genealogists, 2021). Clear labeling does not weaken research. It makes it more durable.

Hidden uncertainty produces fragile conclusions that collapse under scrutiny. Visible uncertainty produces work that can adapt as new evidence appears.

Transparency in Shared Research Spaces

Most Irish genealogy now happens in shared spaces: online trees, collaborative projects, discussion forums, and DNA networks.

In these settings, when hypotheses are clearly labeled, they protect your work, your collaborators, and the people who will build on it later.

When uncertainty is stated openly, others can evaluate the reasoning, contribute evidence, and challenge conclusions without undermining the work.

Moving Forward Without Freezing

Several missteps show up at this stage. Some researchers wait for certainty before acting. Others move forward but present hypotheses as facts. Some treat revision as failure, while others avoid conclusions entirely.

Each response stalls progress in a different way. The correction is the same in every case: move forward with hypotheses, label them clearly, and treat revision as evidence that the method is working.

If You Remember One Thing

Moving forward with clearly labeled hypotheses is responsible practice, not a compromise (Board for Certification of Genealogists, 2021).

Chapter 4: When Absence Is Evidence

Many researchers treat missing records as a dead end. That reaction is understandable. Most research environments train us to expect that effort will always be rewarded with results. A search returns nothing. A register does not include the entry you expected. A database comes up empty. The immediate reaction is often self-doubt: something must have been done wrong, or progress must be blocked.

In Irish genealogy, that assumption often does not hold.

As outlined earlier, when a record doesn't turn up, it can feel like the search failed. In Irish genealogy, a missing record is often just information of a different kind.If you take the time to record what's missing and think about why it's missing, it can help you rule things out and get your research back on track (Bloch, 1953; Trouillot, 1995).

Why Missing Records Are So Common

Irish records contain gaps for many reasons, most of which have nothing to do with researcher error. In some cases, records were never created for certain events or populations. In others, records existed but did not survive because of loss, damage, or administrative change.

Coverage varies sharply by parish, time period, and religious denomination. Civil and church boundaries often do not align cleanly. Even when records survive, indexes may be incomplete or inaccurate.

Because of this, the absence of a record does not automatically mean an event did not occur. It only means the event was not captured, preserved, or indexed in the record set being used.

That distinction matters. Absence is normal in Irish research, and treating it as failure can derail otherwise careful work.This distinction isn't about catching mistakes. It's about making sure absence is carrying the right amount of weight—and not more.

Absence Versus Incomplete Searching

Not every negative result counts as evidence. Absence becomes meaningful only after a search is thorough, appropriately scoped, and documented.

Before treating a missing record as informative, it is necessary to confirm that the correct time frame was searched, the geographic scope was reasonable, name variants and spellings were considered, and the record set is known to exist for the period in question.

If those conditions are not met, the absence reflects incomplete searching rather than evidence.

How Absence Narrows Possibilities

The absence of records doesn't give you answers, but it can help you rule things out (Trouillot, 1995).

If several siblings are baptized in a particular parish and one expected baptism does not appear there, the family may have been living elsewhere at that time. If a surname does not appear in land records for a townland across multiple decades, that location may be excluded from consideration. If a civil record is missing during a period when coverage is known to be complete, information reported in later records may be inaccurate.

In each case, absence does not point to a single conclusion. It limits the field. That narrowing is often what allows progress to resume.

Documenting Negative Searches

Negative searches should be recorded with the same care as positive findings. Without documentation, absence cannot function as evidence. Searches get repeated. Assumptions harden. Time is lost.

A useful research note records what was searched, where it was searched, the time period covered, which variants were considered, and what the result was.

Negative Search Entry (so absence can count as evidence)

When to use: Any time you searched and found "nothing," and you want that nothing to do real work later.

Copy/paste fields (fill in as bullets):

- Next action (1-3 steps):

- Date logged:

- Question being tested:

- Expected event/person:

- Record set searched (exact): (parish register / civil index / land record / newspaper, etc.)

- Where searched: (site + collection name + film/book/volume if applicable)

- Time period covered: (years actually searched)

- Geographic scope: (townland/parish/civil parish/PLU/county-be specific)

- Name forms tried: (spellings, Irish/English forms, initials, wildcards)

- Search method: (browse images / index search / both; filters used)

- Result: (none found / partial / unclear)

- Coverage check: (does the record set exist for this period? known gaps?)

- What this absence might mean (choose one):

- incomplete search (scope too narrow)

- record gap / survival issue

- event occurred elsewhere (adjacent parish/jurisdiction)

- identity assumption may be wrong

Mini-example A: Missing baptism (absence redirects, not "fails")

- Question being tested: Was Mary (Reilly) baptized in Parish X around 1842?

- Record set searched: Parish X baptism register (images + index)

- Time period covered: 1840-1846

- Geographic scope: Parish X; also checked townland spellings

- Name forms tried: Reilly/Riley; Mary/Maria; wildcard R*illy

- Result: No entry located

- Coverage check: Register survives for 1840-1846; handwriting difficult but legible

- What this absence might mean: Event recorded in a neighboring parish OR residence shifted near a boundary

- Next action: Search adjacent parishes tied to the townland; check siblings' baptisms for clustering; check land records to confirm residence

Mini-example B: Missing surname in land records (absence narrows place)

- Question being tested: Does the surname appear in Townland Y across valuation revisions?

- Record set searched: Griffith's Valuation + later revision notes (Townland Y)

- Time period covered: Valuation year + multiple revisions (years noted in images)

- Name forms tried: standard spelling + common variants

- Result: Surname does not appear in Townland Y in any checked revision

- Coverage check: Townland pages intact; neighboring townlands present

- What this absence might mean: Townland Y is unlikely as the family's base; shift focus to adjacent townlands where the surname does appear

- Next action: Map adjacent townlands; search the parish registers tied to those townlands; track neighbors who recur elsewhere

Systematic documentation of negative searches is what careful researchers already do, not an admission that something went wrong (Mills, 2017).

What This Looks Like in Practice

A researcher believes a child was born in a particular parish based on later records. A search of that parish's baptism registers turns up nothing.

Instead of assuming the record is missing or the search was flawed, the researcher confirms that the register survives for that period, expands the search to nearby parishes, and consults land records to see where the family may have been living at the time.

In this case, the absence of a baptism in the expected parish becomes evidence that the family likely lived elsewhere during that period.

The missing record does not solve the problem. It redirects the work.

The Risks of Over-Interpreting Absence

Absence can be misused as easily as it can be ignored.

Common problems include treating absence as proof an event did not occur, overlooking known gaps in record survival, assuming completeness where none exists, or drawing conclusions from a single negative search.

Absence always has to be interpreted within the broader context of record creation, survival, and coverage. Without that context, it turns into speculation rather than evidence.

Common Sticking Points

Several issues show up repeatedly when working with missing records.

Researchers repeat unsuccessful searches because absence was never recorded. Missing records get treated as confirmation of a favored theory. Boundary changes are overlooked, leading to searches in the wrong jurisdiction. Negative results are remembered informally instead of documented.

These problems are corrected by recording negative searches, treating absence as one factor among many, expanding searches to adjacent jurisdictions when appropriate, and keeping a research log that includes unsuccessful efforts.

How This Chapter Fits Into Your Research

In this chapter, the focus is on how absence can narrow research questions, encourages careful documentation of negative searches, and emphasizes historical context when interpreting missing records.

This book isn't trying to say that absence demonstrates events did not occur, eliminate uncertainty, or replace positive evidence with speculation. Absence is a tool, not a shortcut.

If You Remember One Thing

A carefully documented absence can narrow possibilities and guide next steps without pretending to prove anything.

Chapter 5: Why Consistency Beats Every Tool

Most genealogists don't struggle because they lack tools. More often, they struggle because their method shifts every time the tool does. That pattern is understandable. New databases appear. DNA platforms release new features. Interfaces promise better hints or smarter matches. Each change feels like a fresh chance to solve a stubborn problem.

Activity ramps up. Searches multiply. Notes pile up.

What usually doesn't follow is resolution.

This chapter explains why consistency in method matters more than the number of tools you use, and why disciplined repetition is one of the strongest protections against self-deception in genealogy. This is not an argument against technology. It is an argument for method.

Why Tools Can't Fix Thinking Problems

Tools retrieve, sort, and compare information. They do not evaluate reasoning.

When researchers switch tools frequently or adopt new features without stabilizing their underlying method, interpretation starts to drift. Different platforms apply different thresholds. Notes get recorded unevenly. Terminology shifts without intention. Earlier decisions become hard to reconstruct.

Over time, it becomes unclear whether conclusions changed because new evidence appeared or because the method itself changed. Without a stable framework, increased activity can produce confidence that grows faster than accuracy. That's a methodological problem, not a technological one.

Consistency as a Safeguard Against Assumption

Consistency works as a check on unexamined assumptions. When the same criteria are applied repeatedly, patterns become visible and weak conclusions are easier to spot. Consistency makes it possible to compare results over time, revisit earlier decisions with clarity, explain reasoning to others, and recognize when evidence has actually changed.

Without consistency, conclusions can feel persuasive simply because they are recent or because a new tool presents them more confidently. Confidence goes up. Reliability does not.

In genealogy, consistency isn't rigidity. It's deliberate repetition.

Where Consistency Matters Most

Some parts of research are especially vulnerable when standards shift.

Thresholds are one example. Whether you're evaluating DNA matches, acceptable age ranges, or geographic proximity, thresholds have to stay stable if conclusions are going to be comparable over time. If a match is meaningful one day and dismissed the next without explanation, what's usually happening isn't insight. It's inconsistency.

Documentation is another. Notes should reliably record what was found, what was not found, why a conclusion was reached, and what remains uncertain. When note-taking changes from line to line, earlier reasoning becomes hard to evaluate and revision turns into guesswork.

Terminology also matters. Words like proven, likely, possible, and hypothesis shape how conclusions are understood. If those words are used inconsistently, the apparent strength of a conclusion can change even when the evidence hasn't.

The sequence of reasoning benefits from consistency as well. Establishing place before identity, and context before relationship, creates comparable standards across research lines. Skipping steps introduces uneven judgment that's hard to detect later.

Repetition Versus Redundancy

Consistency is not the same thing as repeating the same search endlessly.

Productive repetition means applying the same method to new evidence, reviewing earlier conclusions using the same criteria, and checking whether patterns hold when conditions stay stable. This kind of repetition strengthens conclusions. Agreement accumulates meaning. Contradictions stand out clearly.

Redundant searching burns time without improving understanding. If you can't explain what a repeated search would test differently today, it's probably redundancy.

What This Looks Like in Practice

Example scenario (composite case): Consider a researcher who evaluates DNA matches using the same thresholds over time and records each decision in a consistent format. Over several months, multiple moderate matches recur in the same geographic area.

Because the method stayed stable, that agreement becomes visible and interpretable. If thresholds had shifted or notes were inconsistent, the same pattern might have been dismissed as noise or overstated as proof. Consistency allows evidence to speak without distortion (Kuhn, 1962; Mills, 2017).

Common Pitfalls and Practical Corrections

Several problems show up when method isn't stable. Researchers adopt new tools reactively, apply different standards to different family lines, or place too much confidence in newly released features. Others find they can't reconstruct past decisions because documentation was inconsistent.

These problems aren't fixed by abandoning tools. They're fixed by stabilizing method. Using a small set of tools consistently, applying the same criteria across all lines, revisiting conclusions within an established framework, and standardizing note-taking all restore clarity.

Methods can improve. They just shouldn't drift.

How This Chapter Fits Into Your Research

This chapter emphasizes method over technology, explains how consistency supports transparency, and shows how disciplined repetition reveals patterns that scattered effort hides. It does not recommend specific platforms, argue against innovation, or suggest that methods should never evolve. Improvement should be deliberate. Drift should not.

Putting This Into Practice

Tools assist, but methods decide. Consistency reveals patterns. Inconsistency hides assumptions. Repetition strengthens reasoning. Discipline protects against error.

If you remember one thing from this chapter:
Consistent method protects accuracy far more reliably than any tool, platform, or new feature.

What you should have now:

- A way to resize questions when research stalls

- A method for moving forward without overstating certainty

- Language to label conclusions honestly and responsibly

Up to this point, the focus has been on how to think. From here on, the focus shifts to how Irish records actually behave. The methods you've learned only work if they're applied within the realities of Irish record systems, geography, and daily life.

Deep Dive: Resizing the Question Before You Search

Patrick Reilly is the kind of entry that makes Irish research feel impossible: Born: Ireland. Married: New York. Died: Brooklyn. No parish. No townland. No parents. You can keep searching Irish baptisms for decades and still never find the "right" Patrick Reilly-because the question you're asking is bigger than what the record set can reliably answer at the start.

Using SCALE, the first move is not to search harder. It's to resize. Instead of "Who were Patrick's parents?" the working question becomes: What can I say about Patrick Reilly in Brooklyn that is stable enough to test? That means building a profile from the records that are designed to describe a person's adult life: addresses, occupations, churches, witnesses, sponsors, burial location, the repeated names that appear around him, and the neighborhoods where those names recur.

This does not produce identity in one leap. It produces structure. It turns a vague immigrant into a person who can be placed in a time-and-place network that can later be compared to Irish candidates.

The records allow this much: a better question, grounded in what survives and what records were built to capture. They do not yet allow the one question that feels emotionally urgent: a direct parentage statement. That question comes later-if the structure earns it.

Unit II: Ireland as a Research Environment

The methods in Unit I only work if you accept one central truth: Irish records are products of systems. Records come from systems. They reflect the priorities, boundaries, and blind spots of the institutions that created them.

A practical way to keep that straight is to treat every record as if it is answering three questions:

- Who created this?

- What were they trying to do in that moment?

- What jurisdiction made it official?

If you cannot answer those questions, you are at high risk of misreading what the record can legitimately support.

Ireland's main record systems were built for immediate use, not for family reconstruction. Civil administration tracked events and populations. Churches tracked religious rites and community membership. Land systems tracked tenancy and taxation. Local governance tracked responsibility and obligation.

None of these systems were built to make modern genealogists happy.

That mismatch is why Irish genealogy feels hard. It is not usually because the researcher lacks skill. It is because the records were not designed to answer the kinds of questions we naturally ask today.

Modern expectations- unique identification, clear lineage, consistency across decades- often do not line up with how Irish records were meant to function.

To do Irish research well, you have to understand Ireland as a record-keeping environment, not as a pile of isolated documents.

That is why this unit focuses less on how to search and more on what the record systems themselves make possible and what they routinely leave out. Records reflect institutional priorities, and those priorities shape what gets written down, what gets standardized, and what never appears at all.

When we treat those gaps as personal failure, we misread the archive. When we treat them as features of how history was recorded, we can describe the limits plainly, build stronger inferences, and stop demanding answers the sources were never positioned to provide.

How Irish Life Shaped Irish Records

Irish people did not live their lives by county, even though modern researchers often start there. Daily life ran on smaller, more practical units.

People lived in townlands, attended churches that did not always align with civil boundaries, and moved through landscapes shaped by roads, rivers, estates, and long-standing community ties.

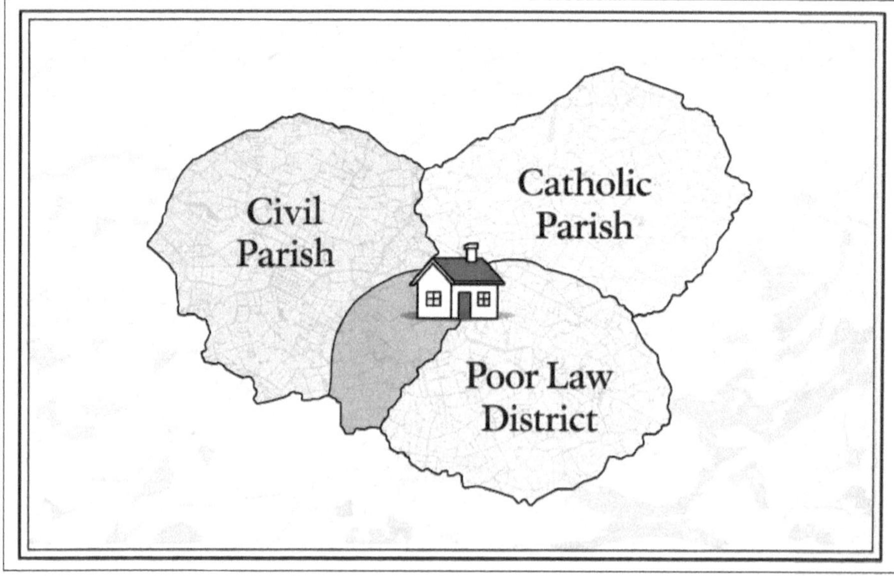

Figure 1. One Place, Multiple Jurisdictions

How Irish Life Shaped Irish Records

A single townland may be described by different administrative systems without describing different places.

Why Place Matters More Than Name

Irish identity was grounded in place and association more than in unique naming (Massey, 1994; Bourdieu, 1977).

Names repeat. Places anchor.

This unit explains how understanding Irish place structures stabilizes research when names alone cannot.

Recalibrating Expectations

This unit does not promise answers. It resets expectations.

Understanding how Irish records behave turns confusion into pattern and frustration into proportion (Braudel, 1980).

The next chapter begins at the most stable level of Irish research: Place.

Chapter 6: Townlands, Parishes, and What "Near" Really Meant

Irish genealogy often succeeds or fails on one thing: place. Many problems that look complicated later come from a simple issue early on. Modern researchers often read Irish locations using today's maps and administrative logic, instead of the lived geography that shaped Irish records.

If you misunderstand the geography, the records can look like they don't match. But once you understand the place correctly, those same records usually make sense.

This chapter lays out how townlands, parishes, and other local divisions worked in everyday Irish life, why modern boundaries can mislead, and what "near" actually meant in a society organized by walking distance rather than neat map lines.

Modern county boundaries are administratively convenient but historically blunt instruments. Counties mattered to government oversight. They mattered far less to daily life.

Townlands, by contrast, functioned as the basic unit of residence, labor, and local identity. They often remained stable even as larger jurisdictions shifted around them. When research begins at the county level, meaningful local patterns are diluted or missed. When it begins at the townland level, records from different systems- church, land, and civil- are far more likely to resolve into a coherent picture.

In practice, "near" is best treated as a route, not a radius. People moved along roads, paths, and familiar travel lines shaped by terrain, rivers, estates, and market towns.

Two locations that look far apart on a modern map may have been near in real life, while two that look adjacent may have been effectively separated. The goal is not to reconstruct every footpath. The goal is to stop treating proximity like geometry and start treating it like access.

Townlands: The Smallest Meaningful Unit

The townland was the basic unit of Irish daily life. Townlands were not abstract divisions on a survey sheet. They were lived spaces: fields, clusters of houses, shared resources, and local work patterns.

People knew them intimately because land, labor, neighbors, and identity were organized at that level. In many places, people described themselves by townland long before they identified with a parish or county.

For genealogy, townlands are often the most stable geographic anchor available. Parishes could shift. Civil jurisdictions could be reorganized. County borders mattered far less in daily life than they do to modern researchers.

When a family appears repeatedly in the same townland across different record types, that continuity is rarely random.

Parishes: Overlapping Systems, Not Neat Layers

Parishes complicate Irish research because there is not a single parish system. Civil parishes, Catholic parishes, Church of Ireland parishes, and chapel districts often overlap imperfectly.

They were shaped by different authorities for different purposes, and they changed on different timelines.

A single townland might sit in one civil parish but be served by a Catholic chapel tied to another. Families often attended the church that was closest or easiest to reach, not the one that aligned neatly with civil boundaries.

As a result, baptisms, marriages, and burials can appear in records that look inconsistent when viewed through a modern map. That pattern often reflects how people actually moved through their local environment.

What "Near" Really Meant

In nineteenth-century Ireland, "near" usually meant walkable.

Distance was measured by time and terrain, not by straight lines. Roads, rivers, hills, estates, and established travel routes shaped where people went to church, registered events, and interacted socially.

When records place related events in neighboring parishes or adjacent townlands, that pattern often reflects practical geography rather than contradiction.

How Misunderstanding Place Creates False Problems

Many research frustrations come from treating modern administrative units as if they controlled historical behavior.

Searching whole counties can bury the local patterns that matter most. Expecting all events to appear in one parish ignores overlapping jurisdictions. Treating parish boundaries as fixed assumes stability that did not exist.

When place is misunderstood, records look contradictory. When place is reconstructed accurately, many of those contradictions disappear.

Reconstructing Local Geography

Effective Irish research often requires rebuilding local geography as it existed in the period being studied.

That usually means identifying the townland first, determining which civil and religious jurisdictions served it at the time, and thinking about how people would have moved through that landscape.

The 15-Minute Townland-First Workflow (reconstruct local geography fast)

Goal: Turn "place" from a label into a search plan you can repeat.

Step 1 - Capture the place exactly as written

- Copy the location string verbatim from every record (including "near," "outside," and abbreviations).

Step 2 - Identify the smallest stable anchor

- If you have a townland, start there.

- If you only have a parish/county, list candidate townlands later-don't pretend you have one yet.

Step 3 - Build a "jurisdiction stack" (in bullets, not a table)

- Townland:

- Civil parish:

- Religious parish/chapel likely used:

- Barony / Poor Law Union / Registration district (if relevant to your target records):

Step 4 - Build a "walkable set"

- List the adjacent townlands and neighboring parishes most accessible by roads/terrain (treat "near" as access, not geometry).

Step 5 - Choose your search order

- Search the most plausible parish/register first, then expand outward in the walkable set.

- Log each expansion as a deliberate step (not a panic spiral).

Step 6 - Write a one-line working rule

- Example: "For this family, I will treat events within adjacent parishes as plausible until evidence rules them out."

Boundary decision bullets (use when records appear in "the wrong parish")

- If events appear in two neighboring parishes, assume boundary behavior first (chapel access, seasonal movement, landlord estates) before assuming two families.

- If baptisms are missing in the "right" parish, check whether the family is on the edge of two catchments (civil vs Catholic overlaps).

- If one record names a place once and it never appears again, treat it as a clue to test, not a conclusion to build on.

- If the only "place" is a county, treat county as a container, not an origin-reduce it using townlands tied to cluster families, neighbors, sponsors, or land anchors.

Micro-example (what this looks like)

- Record A places a baptism in Parish 1; Record B places a sibling in Parish 2.

- Instead of splitting the family, you build the jurisdiction stack from the townland, map the walkable set, then search both parish registers as overlapping coverage.

The goal is not perfect cartographic precision. It is functional understanding, enough to judge whether records plausibly belong to the same family operating within a shared local environment.

What This Looks Like in Practice

A researcher finds a family appearing in baptism records from two neighboring parishes and assumes the records belong to different families.

Later, a closer look at townland boundaries shows the family lived near the edge of both parish catchments, and the most accessible chapel changed over time.

What looked like inconsistency was continuity.

How This Chapter Fits Into Your Research

This chapter provides a working understanding of townlands and parishes, explains why modern maps can mislead, and shows how to interpret proximity the way people lived it.

This book isn't trying to say that geography alone resolves identity. Place is the foundation that keeps later conclusions from wobbling.

If You Remember One Thing

Place in Irish genealogy is lived and layered, and understanding how people moved locally resolves many apparent contradictions.

Chapter 7: When the Same Name Is Not the Same Person

It's very tempting to assume that a shared name means a shared identity. In Irish genealogy, that assumption is one of the quickest ways a tree can quietly go off course. In Irish records, that assumption fails more often than it works.

Irish naming patterns reuse names on purpose. Names repeat within families and communities, and name alone is rarely sufficient to establish identity (Bloch, 1953; Fischer, 1970). Given names followed cultural traditions. Surnames clustered by location. In many communities, several people with the same name lived at the same time, often within walking distance of one another.

Modern expectations of name uniqueness do not apply.

Here, the focus is on why name-based identification breaks down so often in Irish genealogy, how premature merging creates long-term error, and why keeping people separate longer than feels comfortable is one of the strongest accuracy safeguards available.

Why Name Reuse Was Normal

Irish naming patterns were deliberate, not accidental. Children were often named after parents, grandparents, or close relatives. The same given names repeat across generations within the same families.

In small populations, the pool of surnames was limited, and the pool of given names even more so. Finding multiple people with the same name in the same parish or townland is expected.

Irish records were not designed to reliably distinguish between same-named individuals. Ages, occupations, and parentage are often missing or inconsistently recorded.

Expecting records to separate identities by name alone asks them to do work they were never meant to do.

The Cost of Premature Merging

Many people merge early because they're trying to make sense of limited information. That instinct is understandable- even when it causes problems later. Merging records too quickly creates problems that often do not show up right away.

Timelines stretch. Ages drift. Events overlap. Small contradictions get explained away instead of examined.

Over time, the merged identity becomes harder to untangle. Errors spread into shared trees, DNA interpretations, and published work. What started as a shortcut turns into long-term cleanup.

Once individuals are merged, researchers tend to defend the conclusion instead of testing it. Revision becomes costly. Confidence increases while accuracy declines.

Separation as a way to keep from jumping to conclusions

If keeping people separate feels uncomfortable or unfinished, that reaction is normal. Irish records rarely reward quick closure. Keeping same-named individuals separate is not indecision. It is a deliberate safeguard.

Separation allows evidence to accumulate independently. It preserves alternative explanations. It keeps contradictions visible instead of forcing them into a single story.

In Irish research, it is almost always safer to keep two people separate longer than feels comfortable than to merge them prematurely.

What Actually Distinguishes Individuals

In Irish genealogy, people are distinguished less by name and more by continuity.

Continuity of place matters most. Individuals who appear repeatedly in the same townland, interact with the same neighbors, attend the same church, and remain within a consistent geographic range are far more likely to represent the same person than individuals connected only by name.

Continuity of association matters as well. Recurring sponsors, witnesses, neighbors, and landholders form identifiable clusters.

Chronology provides another constraint. Events must fit within plausible lifespans, family formation patterns, and historical context. When timelines strain credibility, identity should be questioned.

Names alone are weak identifiers.

What This Looks Like in Practice

A researcher finds two baptism records naming a father called Patrick Reilly in neighboring parishes within the same decade.

Assuming there could only be one such man, the researcher merges the records into a single family.

Later, land records show two Patrick Reillys holding land in adjacent townlands at the same time. Sponsors differ. Burial records overlap.

What once felt efficient now requires undoing years of compounded assumption.

If the individuals had been kept separate from the start, the evidence would have clarified their distinct identities on its own.

Letting Identity Emerge

Rather than asking whether this is the same person, a more useful question is whether this record fits the same place, associations, and timeline as the others.

When enough answers line up, identity becomes a supported conclusion rather than a leap.

How This Chapter Fits Into Your Research

In this chapter, you'll see why same-name confusion is routine in Irish records, why Premature merging makes later interpretation less stable, and how deliberate separation protects interpretation.

It argues for sequence: Structure first, identity after.

If You Remember One Thing

Names repeat by design in Irish records, and identity emerges from continuity of place and association, not from name alone.

A helpful way to keep this sequence clear is PLACE:

- Put people in a location first
- Look for repetition over time
- Attend to associations such as neighbors, sponsors, and witnesses
- Constrain conclusions with chronology
- Emerge identity last, once structure is in place

PLACE helps resist the urge to merge too early and keeps interpretation grounded when names alone confuse more than they clarify.

P	Put people in a location first
L	Look for repetition over time
A	Attend to associations
C	Constrain conclusions with chronology
E	Emerge identity last

Chapter 8: Land Records as Anchors, Not Answers

Land records rarely say what researchers most want them to say. They usually do not name parents. They seldom describe relationships. Ages, origins, and reasons for change are often missing.

For anyone hoping for direct confirmation of family connections, Irish land records can feel frustratingly indirect.

And yet, they are some of the most reliable tools available in Irish genealogy.

In this chapter, you'll see how to use land records not as answers to genealogical questions, but as anchors: fixed points in time and place that stabilize research when other records are sparse, missing, or ambiguous.

What Irish Land Records Were Designed to Do

Irish land records were created to manage property, taxation, and tenancy, not to document family relationships.

Sources such as the Tithe Applotment Books, Griffith's Valuation, and estate records were designed to identify who held or occupied land, where that land was located, and how it was assessed. Their purpose was administrative and economic.

Any genealogical value they offer is incidental. Expecting land records to explain family relationships misunderstands why they exist.

Why Land Records Matter Anyway

Despite their limits, land records do one thing exceptionally well: They hold people still.

They place named individuals in specific townlands at specific moments. They show who lived near whom. They reveal continuity, replacement, and disappearance.

When tracked over time, they can suggest persistence across generations even when relationships are never stated.

In an environment where names repeat and church records may be incomplete, this stability matters.

Continuity, Replacement, and Absence

One of the most useful features of land records is their ability to show change over time.

When the same surname appears on the same holding across multiple valuation revisions, it suggests long-term residence. When one name disappears and another appears in its place, it suggests succession, migration, or death, even if the reason is not recorded.

When a surname never appears where it was expected, that absence can narrow possibilities.

These patterns do not prove relationships. They create limits. Any proposed relationship has to fit within them.

Neighbors as Context

Land records are especially valuable when reading sideways instead of in isolation.

Families rarely lived alone. Neighbors listed in land records often reappear as baptism sponsors, marriage witnesses, or burial plot holders.

When the same clusters of names appear together across different record types and over time, identification becomes more stable.

A shared surname means very little on its own. Shared place and repeated proximity mean much more.

What Land Records Cannot Tell You

Land records cannot reliably separate same-named individuals by themselves.

They cannot explain why a tenancy changed. They cannot confirm parent-child relationships. They cannot assign identity without help from other sources.

Using land records as answers leads to overinterpretation. Using them as anchors gives other evidence something solid to attach to.

What This Looks Like in Practice

A researcher finds a Patrick Reilly listed in Griffith's Valuation in a particular townland. Baptism records from the nearby parish show Patrick Reilly acting repeatedly as a sponsor.

Later valuation revisions show the holding passing to another Reilly. No document explains how these individuals are related.

A rushed approach assumes father-to-son succession and moves on. A disciplined approach treats the land record as an anchor. It fixes place, time, and association while leaving the relationship open as a working assumption to be tested against additional evidence.

The difference is not caution for its own sake. It is measured against the strength of the records.

Integrating Land Records Responsibly

Land records work best as part of a system.

They anchor timelines. They limit geographic assumptions. They help distinguish between same-named individuals by showing who was present where and when.

They give context that makes church records, civil records, and DNA evidence interpretable rather than isolated.

Their value comes from integration, not from standing alone.

How This Chapter Fits Into Your Research

Here, the focus is on how Irish land records function, why they are structurally reliable, and how they support research without stretching the evidence.

It does not suggest that land records solve identity questions, replace church registers, or eliminate uncertainty. Their value lies in stability, not completeness.

If You Remember One Thing

Land records stabilize research by anchoring people in place and time, even when they cannot name relationships.

Chapter 9: Reading Sideways: Neighbors, Sponsors, and Witnesses

Irish genealogy rarely moves in a straight line. When direct evidence is thin, progress often comes from looking sideways instead of upward, at the people who appear repeatedly around an individual, rather than at the individual alone. Irish genealogy often moves sideways before it moves up (Ginzburg, 1989).

Neighbors, baptism sponsors, marriage witnesses, and burial choices form patterns of association that persist even when explicit relationships are never written down.

Here, the focus is on how looking at neighbors, not just direct line works in Irish research, why it is often more reliable than name-based identification, and how repeated proximity can distinguish individuals without forcing conclusions.

Why Relationships Are Often Indirect

Irish records rarely explain relationships in the way modern researchers expect.

Sponsors are listed without explanation. Witnesses appear without context. Neighbors recur across different records with no description of how they are connected.

This is not carelessness. It reflects how records were designed.

Irish record-keepers assumed local knowledge. Relationships were understood within the community and did not need to be spelled out for administrative or religious purposes. What mattered was presence, participation, and responsibility, not explanation for future readers.

What survives is pattern rather than statement.

The Power of Repetition

A single sponsor or witness proves nothing. Repetition does.

When the same names recur across baptisms, marriages, land records, and burial registers within the same place and time frame, a network of associations begins to emerge.

These networks are often more stable than individual details such as age or stated origin, which may vary or be missing altogether.

Repetition turns coincidence into structure.

Neighbors as Evidence

Neighbors are not incidental in Irish records.

Families lived close together, worked nearby land, attended the same churches, and interacted daily. Over time, those relationships show up across record types.

Neighbors listed in land records often reappear as baptism sponsors or marriage witnesses. Burial choices may reflect the same local ties.

When the same cluster of surnames appears repeatedly alongside an individual across multiple records, those associations carry weight even when relationships are never defined.

Reading Sideways Without Overreaching

Looking at neighbors, not just direct lines does not name relationships. It suggests continuity.

The goal is not to declare how people were related, but to observe who consistently appears together, where, and when.

Overreaching happens when association is treated as proof rather than pattern. Careful reading keeps conclusions in line with what the records show.

What This Looks Like in Practice

A researcher notices that the same neighbors appear repeatedly as sponsors for multiple children in one family and as witnesses in related marriage records.

Rather than assuming kinship, the researcher records the pattern, tracks the neighbors across land records, and notes continued proximity over time.

That pattern strengthens confidence that the records belong to the same family operating within a stable local network, even without explicit statements of relationship.

Limits of Looking at Neighbors, Not Just Direct Lines

Sideways evidence cannot, by itself, prove parentage or precise relationships.

Associations can change. Communities evolve. Some proximity is coincidental.

Looking at neighbors, not just direct line works best when combined with place, chronology, and other record types. Used alone, it can mislead. Integrated carefully, it stabilizes identification.

How This Chapter Fits into Your Research

What follows lays out how neighbors, sponsors, and witnesses can be used as indirect evidence without overstating their meaning.

It emphasizes repetition, context, and restraint. Sideways reading supports structure. It does not replace documentation.

If You Remember One Thing

Repeated association within the same place and time often tells you more than names alone.

Chapter 10: When the Record Really Isn't There

Some records never existed. Others existed but did not survive. In Irish genealogy, knowing the difference matters.

Many researchers continue searching long after a record can reasonably be expected to appear. Databases are rechecked. Indexes are revisited. New platforms are tried. When nothing turns up, the assumption is often that the search was flawed or incomplete.

In many cases, the problem is not the search. It is the expectation.

In this chapter, you'll see how to recognize when a record genuinely does not exist or no longer survives, how to stop searching responsibly, and how to pivot without filling gaps with speculation.

Records That Never Existed

Not every life event was recorded in Ireland, and not every population was covered even when records existed.

Before civil registration, many events left no official trace. Church records vary by denomination, parish, and period. Some congregations kept minimal registers. Others recorded selectively. Some events were never written down at all.

Expecting a record to exist when it never could have leads to wasted effort and unnecessary doubt.

Records That Did Not Survive

Some records were created but no longer exist.

Loss occurred through fire, decay, neglect, administrative disposal, and political upheaval. Survival varies sharply by place and record type.

A missing record in a parish with known gaps carries different meaning than a missing record where coverage is otherwise complete. Knowing survival patterns is essential to interpretation.

Recognizing When Searching Is No Longer Productive

A search becomes unproductive when it no longer tests a new idea.

If the same sources have been searched repeatedly with the same parameters, and no new expectations are being evaluated, continued searching adds effort without information.

Knowing when to stop searching isn't quitting. Stopping one kind of search often creates space for a better one. It's a shift in direction, not an end to the work. It usually means you're ready to shift direction and ask better questions.

What to Do Instead of Searching

When a record is unlikely to exist, the work shifts.

Instead of searching harder, researchers can document absence, reassess assumptions, narrow geographic focus, or move sideways into other record types. Land records, association patterns, migration clusters, and later-life documents may provide structure even when early records do not.

Progress often comes from changing direction, not increasing intensity.

The Risk of Filling Gaps

When records are missing, the temptation to fill gaps is strong.

Researchers may infer relationships, origins, or timelines without sufficient support. These inferences can feel reasonable, especially when they complete a story.

But filling gaps without evidence weakens the work. It replaces uncertainty with confidence that cannot be defended or revised.

How This Looks Like in Practice

A researcher expects to find a baptism record for a child born in the early nineteenth century in a specific parish. Multiple searches turn up nothing.

Rather than assuming the record must exist and continuing to search indefinitely, the researcher checks parish coverage, confirms known gaps, and documents the negative result.

Attention then shifts to land records and later-life documents to establish residence and association instead of birth details.

The work continues without pretending the missing record will appear.

How This Chapter Fits into Your Research

Here, the focus is on helping you recognize when continued searching no longer produces new information, teaches how to document absence responsibly, and explains how to pivot without speculation.

It does not argue that searching is futile or that records should not be pursued thoroughly. It argues for proportional effort and honest limits.

If You Remember One Thing

Knowing when to stop searching is a research skill, not a shortcoming.

Deep Dive: Place Anchors, Not Name Matches

By the end of Unit II, the Reilly problem looks different-not solved, but more stable. The goal here is not to "find Patrick in Ireland." The goal is to learn what Irish records will let you do without forcing them to declare identity.

This is where PLACE matters. If a Patrick Reilly candidate appears in Irish records, the temptation is to merge him immediately: same name, plausible date, maybe even a parish that "sounds right." Unit II teaches you to do the opposite. You anchor the Irish candidate to place first-townland, parish system, adjacent jurisdictions, and the small set of families who appear repeatedly alongside him.

Instead of asking "Is this my Patrick?", you ask smaller, testable questions:

- Does the same Reilly household repeat in the same townland across land and church sources?

- Do the same sponsors or witnesses recur across baptisms and marriages in that local area?

- Do boundaries explain apparent contradictions (civil parish vs Catholic parish vs registration district), or are you mixing two different places?

This is also where you stop searching for records that cannot exist or cannot survive. Documented absence becomes part of the reasoning instead of a private frustration.

The records allow a disciplined claim: "This Patrick Reilly belongs to this local network in this place." They do not yet allow: "This is the immigrant in Brooklyn." PLACE is how you keep those statements from collapsing into each other.

Unit III: Crossing the Atlantic Without Stretching the Evidence

Migration is where many Irish research errors harden into certainty. That pressure doesn't come from carelessness. It comes from wanting resolution after a long, difficult search.

Once families appear outside Ireland, the temptation to resolve origins quickly becomes strong. Passenger lists, census entries, and death records feel like they should provide answers that Irish records did not.

Often, they do not.

This unit explains how to work with diaspora records responsibly, how to recognize patterns without overstating them, and how to prevent migration evidence from being asked to do more than it can support.

Irish migration followed people, not paperwork. Understanding that changes how destination records should be read.

Arrival records capture movement. Settlement records capture the community. Neither reliably declares origin on its own.

When diaspora evidence is treated as structure rather than proof, it becomes one of the strongest tools available.

This unit focuses on migration chains, settlement clusters, and record systems outside Ireland, with an emphasis on proportional conclusions and clearly labeled uncertainty.

Patterns guide research. They do not end it.

Chapter 11: Migration Chains and Settlement Clusters

Irish migration did not happen at random. People rarely left alone, arrived alone, or settled without connection. Irish families rarely migrated alone (Bodnar, 1985; Diner, 1983). Movement followed paths already worn by others.

Understanding those paths changes how migration evidence should be read.

What follows lays out how migration chains and settlement clusters functioned, why they matter more than isolated passenger records, and how patterns of arrival and settlement can provide structure when direct origin evidence is missing.

Why Migration Was Rarely Individual

Leaving Ireland required money, information, and support. Most migrants relied on family members, neighbors, or acquaintances who had already made the journey.

Letters, remittances, and word of mouth guided decisions about when to leave, where to land, and where to settle. New arrivals often stayed with people they already knew or with others from the same area.

As a result, migration tends to cluster. People from the same townlands, parishes, or neighboring areas often appear together in destination records.

Treating migration as an individual event ignores how movement actually worked.

Settlement Was the Second Half of Migration

Arrival was only the beginning. Settlement patterns mattered just as much.

Irish immigrants often settled near others from the same places. Settlement patterns abroad often reflect pre-existing ties rather than random distribution (Bodnar, 1985). Churches, neighborhoods, workplaces, and burial grounds reflected those connections. Over time, these clusters became stable communities tied to specific places of origin.

Looking only at passenger lists misses this second half of the story. Settlement records often preserve patterns that arrival records do not.

Why Clusters Matter More Than Single Records

A single migration record rarely identifies origin clearly. Many passenger lists list only a country. Some list nothing at all.

Clusters, by contrast, accumulate detail.

When several people from the same destination community trace back to a shared parish or region, that pattern carries weight. When neighbors in Ireland appear as neighbors again abroad, continuity strengthens.

Clusters do not establish origin on their own. Contemporary migration scholarship continues to emphasize that chain migration produces patterned movement without guaranteeing shared origin or kinship.Recent work in migration studies continues to stress that clusters reflect opportunity, access, and social pathways rather than precise identity (Morawska, 2001). For genealogical research, this distinction is critical. Clusters are best understood as structures that narrow questions and guide testing, not as evidence that resolves identity on their own. Treating migration patterns as probabilistic context rather than confirmation preserves their analytical value without overstating what they can support. They narrow possibilities and provide context that makes later evidence interpretable.

Recognizing Migration Chains

Migration chains often appear through repetition.

Shared surnames appear together in arrival records. The same witnesses or sponsors show up in destination church records. Families settle near one another across decades. Burial plots group people who arrived separately but lived communally.

These patterns point back toward shared origin areas even when no document names them explicitly.

Mistakes That Break Cluster Analysis

Several patterns commonly weaken cluster-based research.

Researchers focus on one individual instead of the surrounding group. They merge unrelated people because they arrived on the same ship. They ignore settlement records in favor of arrival documents. They assume proximity proves kinship.

Cluster analysis works only when patterns are tracked carefully and conclusions remain proportional.

What This Looks Like in Practice

A researcher studies an Irish immigrant who settled in New York but cannot identify a parish of origin. Passenger records provide no usable detail.

Looking sideways, the researcher examines neighbors in census records, baptism sponsors, and marriage witnesses. Several of these families trace back to the same small region in Ireland.

That pattern does not prove the immigrant came from that place. It makes that place plausible and worth testing against Irish records.

How This Chapter Fits Into Your Research

If you've ever found yourself wondering how migration chains and settlement clusters create structure in diaspora research.

This book isn't trying to say that clusters replace documentary proof or guarantee origin. It shows how they narrow questions, guide searching, and prevent saying more than the records support when direct evidence is missing.

If You Remember One Thing

Irish migration followed people, not paperwork, and clusters often preserve what individual records omit.

Chapter 12: New York Records as a System, not a List

New York records are often treated as a checklist. Researchers move from census to passenger list to civil registration, hoping one of them will finally reveal an Irish place of origin.

That approach is understandable, and it often fails.

New York records work best when they are read as a system rather than as isolated documents.

New York Record System Profile (one person, many record voices)

Goal: Stop asking "Which record is right?" and start asking "What pattern repeats across independent sources?"

Start a profile card (copy/paste):

- Target person (name forms):

- Likely time window in NY:

- Known address/ward/parish/neighborhood:

- Known associates (witnesses, sponsors, neighbors):

- Working origin hypothesis (if any): (leave blank if none)

Then add record cards (repeat as needed):

Census card

- Year:

- Address/ED/ward:

- Birthplace field says:

- Who likely answered:

- What this supports (1 line):

Marriage card

- Date/place:

- Parents named?

- Witnesses:

- Residence at marriage:

- Birthplace/origin field:

- What this supports (1 line):

Death card

- Date/place:

- Informant (if named):

- Birthplace/origin field:

- Residence at death:

- Cemetery:

- What this supports (1 line):

Church card (baptisms/marriages/burials)

- Parish:

- Sponsors/witnesses:

- Recurring surnames:

- What this supports (1 line):

Naturalization card (if present)

- Date/court:
- Arrival details:
- Origin details (if any):
- What this supports (1 line):

Passenger/arrival card (if present)

- Port/date:
- Companions:
- Last residence vs origin wording:
- What this supports (1 line):

How to weigh conflicts (fast rules)

- A single record rarely settles origin. Agreement across independent records adds weight.
- Later records may contain more narrative but weaker memory; earlier records may be blunt but closer to events.
- Treat place-of-origin fields as claims to test unless they repeat through separate channels (church + cemetery + neighbors + multiple documents).

Micro-example (pattern thinking)

- Death record names "County Cavan." Census says only "Ireland." Marriage gives no origin.
- Working move: treat "County Cavan" as a testable hypothesis, then check whether sponsors, witnesses, burial clustering, or neighborhood ties repeatedly connect the person to others tied to that county. If the county appears only once, keep it tentative; if it repeats in independent places, it strengthens.

Each record type reflects a different institutional purpose. When those purposes are understood, the records begin to reinforce one another instead of contradicting each other.

If New York records have ever felt like a pile of contradictions-different answers from different offices-this chapter shows how to read them as a system that produces pattern, not certainty.

Why New York Records Feel Inconsistent

New York records were created by different institutions at different times for different reasons.

Census records aimed to count populations. Civil records documented legal events. Church records tracked religious rites. Immigration records tracked movement, not identity.

Because these systems were not designed to work together, details often conflict. Ages vary. Birthplaces shift. Names change spelling. Information reported decades after an event may be approximate or wrong.

Looking at each record on its own can be confusing. But when you see how they relate to each other, they start to make more sense.

Understanding Informants and Timing

Much of what appears in New York records depends on who provided the information and when.

Birth records are usually reported close to the event. Death records may rely on grieving relatives or distant informants. Census entries reflect whoever happened to answer the enumerator's questions.

Later records often compress memory. Earlier records capture immediacy but less context.

Knowing this helps weigh conflicts without treating them as fatal.

Place of Origin Versus Place of Last Residence

One of the most persistent misunderstandings in New York research involves Irish origin.

Many records report the last place a person lived rather than the place they were born. Some record county or province loosely. Others use "Ireland" as a default.

Assuming every place reference points to birthplace leads to false conclusions. Treating place references as contextual clues rather than declarations keeps interpretation grounded.

Patterns Across Records

A single record rarely clarifies origin. Patterns across records often do.

When the same place appears repeatedly across independent records, confidence increases. When places vary but stay within a region, boundaries may be soft rather than contradictory.

When a place appears once and never again, it may reflect error rather than truth.

The goal is not to find a perfect record. It is to assess agreement.

Common Missteps in New York Research

Several habits undermine otherwise solid work.

Researchers privilege passenger lists over all other sources. They discard records that do not match a favored conclusion. They assume accuracy increases over time. They merge individuals based on partial overlap.

These missteps are corrected by reading records comparatively, not hierarchically.

What This Looks Like in Practice

A researcher finds a death record naming County Cavan as place of birth. Census records list only Ireland. A marriage record gives no origin.

Instead of treating the death record as definitive, the researcher asks whether that county appears elsewhere. Sponsors and witnesses connect the family to others from the same area. Burial records show clustering in a parish associated with immigrants from that county.

The place reference gains weight through agreement, not assertion.

How This Chapter Fits Into Your Research

If you've ever found yourself wondering how to read New York records as an interconnected system, how to weigh inconsistencies without panic, and how to let patterns guide interpretation.

It does not promise that New York records will name Irish origins clearly. It shows how they can narrow possibilities responsibly.

If You Remember One Thing

New York records clarify Irish origins through patterns and agreement, not through single authoritative statements.

Chapter 13: Last Place Seen Is Not Place of Origin

One of the most persistent errors in Irish diaspora research is treating the last place a person lived as the place they came from. Records often preserve the final stop before migration more clearly than the origin itself.

That distinction matters. Misreading this is incredibly common, especially when records finally seem to offer a place name.

If you've ever found yourself wondering why last residence is frequently mistaken for birthplace or origin, how migration within Ireland complicates interpretation, and how to keep movement from being misread as identity.

Why Last Residence Shows Up More Often Than Origin

Many records capture where someone was living at the time of an event, not where they were born.

Marriage records, emigration documents, poor law records, and even some church registers record residence because it mattered administratively. Birthplace often did not.

As a result, a place named in a record may reflect where someone lived shortly before leaving Ireland rather than where their family originated.

Treating every place reference as an origin freezes movement that was often fluid.

Internal Migration Before Emigration

By the nineteenth century, many Irish people had already moved internally before emigrating.

Economic pressure, land subdivision, eviction, seasonal labor, and family networks pushed people from rural townlands into nearby towns, estates, or counties before they ever left Ireland.

When emigration occurred, the recorded place often reflected this last location rather than a deeper familial origin.

Ignoring internal migration compresses complex movement into a single misleading point.

How Misreading Last Residence Creates False Certainty

When a place appears in a record, it feels solid. Researchers want to anchor conclusions quickly.

But anchoring too early creates fragile trees.

Assuming a listed county or parish is a place of origin can send research into the wrong records, generate apparent contradictions, and lead to premature conclusions that later evidence cannot support.

Separating residence from origin keeps interpretation flexible.

Tracing Backward Through Movement

A more reliable approach is to treat the last recorded place as a starting point rather than an endpoint.

From that place, research can move backward: Identifying how long the family appears there, whether earlier records exist elsewhere, and whether associations point to another location.

Movement leaves traces when followed carefully.

Patterns of association often persist even as locations change. Neighbors move together. Sponsors reappear across parishes. Land records show entry and exit points.

Following those patterns reveals structure that a single place name cannot.

What This Looks Like in Practice

A New York death record names a specific Irish county as birthplace. Earlier census records list only Ireland. No Irish baptism appears in that county.

Instead of assuming the record is wrong or continuing to search blindly, the researcher treats the named county as a last residence candidate.

Land records and parish registers in that county show the family arriving shortly before emigration. Earlier records place related families in a neighboring county.

The place named in the death record was real. It just was not the origin.

How This Chapter Fits Into Your Research

If you've ever found yourself wondering why last residence is often mistaken for origin, how internal migration shapes the records, and how to interpret place references without freezing movement.

It does not argue that places listed in records are meaningless. It argues that their meaning depends on timing and context.

If You Remember One Thing

The last place a person lived is often easier to record than the place they came from, and confusing the two distorts research.

Chapter 14: Diaspora Clusters as Clues, Not Proof

When Irish records fail to name an origin directly, researchers often turn to the diaspora for answers. That instinct is reasonable. It can also be dangerous.

Diaspora clusters can preserve valuable information about shared origin, movement, and community ties. They can also amplify error when patterns are assumed to mean more than they do.

If you've ever found yourself wondering how diaspora clusters function as clues rather than proof, how to use them responsibly, and how to keep indirect agreement from turning into stretching the evidence.

What Diaspora Clusters Actually Represent

Diaspora clusters form because people move with people.

Immigrants often settled near relatives, neighbors, or others from the same general area. Churches, workplaces, boarding houses, and neighborhoods reinforced those connections over time.

As a result, destination communities often contain people who share geography, culture, and sometimes kinship. What they do not automatically share is precise origin.

Clusters reflect proximity and connection, not guaranteed identity.

Why Clusters Feel Persuasive

Clusters feel convincing because they create agreement.

When several people in a destination community trace back to the same county or parish, that repetition feels like confirmation. The more often a place appears, the stronger it seems.

But repetition alone does not establish accuracy. Errors can repeat just as easily as truths, especially when early assumptions spread through shared trees, oral tradition, or copied records.

Clusters increase confidence. Confidence feels good, especially after uncertainty. The challenge is learning when to pause and test it. They do not automatically increase correctness.

Using Clusters to Narrow, Not Declare

The most responsible use of diaspora clusters is narrowing.

When multiple families in a destination community point toward the same region, that region becomes plausible. It becomes worth testing against Irish records. It becomes a candidate, not a conclusion.

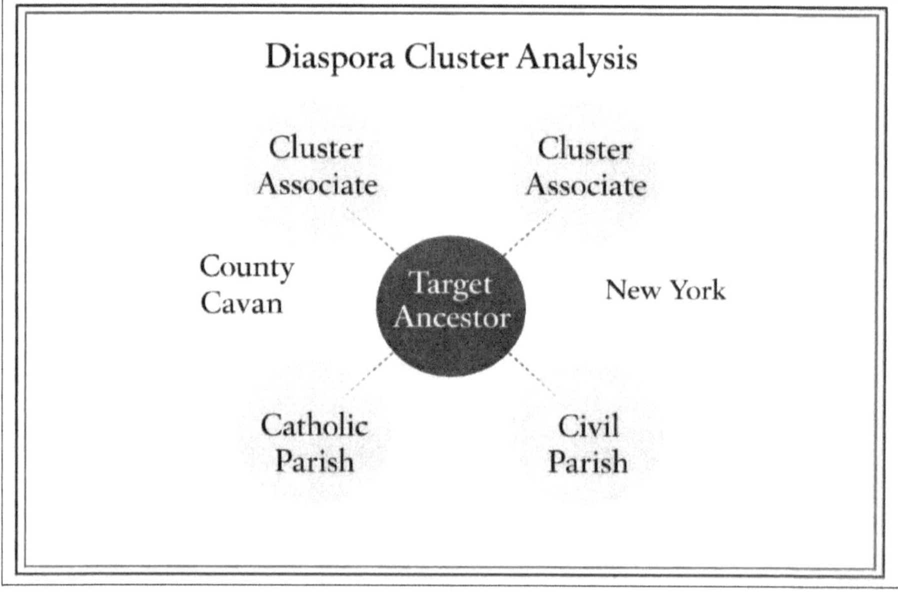

Figure 2. Diaspora Cluster Analysis (Schematic)

A schematic showing how repeated neighbors/associates in destination records form clusters that help narrow an origin question into a testable geographic hypothesis—likely represented as grouped nodes/boxes or a simple flow from broad → narrow.

Separating Shared Place from Shared Family

Not everyone in a cluster is related.

People from neighboring townlands may settle together abroad without sharing kinship. Families may intermarry after migration, creating new ties that did not exist in Ireland. Surnames may cluster geographically without implying relationship.

Assuming kinship based on cluster membership alone collapses distinction that Irish research depends on.

Structure matters more than story.

What This Looks Like in Practice

A researcher studies an immigrant whose Irish origin is unknown. Several families in the same New York parish trace their roots to County Cavan.

Rather than assigning that county as origin, the researcher treats it as a working region. Irish records from that county are tested. Townlands connected to known cluster families are mapped. Associations are tracked.

If Irish records support the connection, confidence increases. If they do not, the cluster remains informative without dictating the conclusion.

Clusters guide questions. They do not answer them.

How This Chapter Fits into Your Research

If you've ever found yourself wondering how diaspora clusters can narrow possibilities without stretching the evidence, how repetition can mislead when not grounded in Irish evidence, and how to integrate destination patterns responsibly.

It does not argue against cluster analysis. It argues for proportional interpretation.

If You Remember One Thing

Diaspora clusters are clues that guide research, not proof that replaces evidence.

Deep Dive: Crossing the Atlantic Without Declaring Victory

Unit III is where the Reilly problem becomes tempting again-because diaspora records feel like they should give you what Ireland didn't. Passenger lists, census entries, and death records seem like they should name the townland, the parish, the parents, the clean origin story. Sometimes they do. Often, they don't.

So the task is to use diaspora evidence as structure, not as a shortcut. You build a "Reilly-in-Brooklyn" profile that treats New York records as a system: the same address appearing across decades, the same church turning up in baptisms and marriages, the same cluster of sponsors or witnesses moving through the records together. This is how you convert "Ireland" into a narrower, testable geography.

Clusters matter here-but only in the way this unit defines them. If several families in Patrick's orbit repeatedly point toward the same region, that region becomes a working region, not a declared origin. It is a candidate that earns testing back in Ireland.

This is also where you protect yourself from "false agreement." When multiple trees say Patrick is from a particular county, that repetition can reflect copying rather than independent support. Unit III keeps you from treating popularity as proof.

The records allow you to say: "Patrick's Brooklyn network overlaps with a set of families whose origins converge on a particular region." They do not allow you to say: "Therefore Patrick came from there." The purpose of Unit III is to narrow the field without closing it prematurely.

Unit IV: DNA, Trees, and Conclusions that Stand Up to Scrutiny

The final stage of Irish research often feels like the most powerful and the most dangerous.

DNA results arrive with numbers and charts. Trees fill in visually. Conclusions feel close.

This is where restraint matters most.

This unit explains how to integrate DNA without letting it override structure, how to use trees as working hypotheses rather than declarations, and how to reach conclusions that remain accurate when shared, copied, and challenged.

Evidence does not speak for itself. It has to be interpreted, weighed, and labeled.

Careful conclusions are not weaker conclusions. They are conclusions that survive scrutiny, revision, and time.

This unit focuses on discipline: Slowing down, maintaining consistency, and choosing clarity over certainty.

Chapter 15: DNA as Supporting Evidence, Not an Answer

DNA testing has transformed Irish genealogy. For many researchers, it feels like a breakthrough after years of uncertainty. Numbers, charts, and shared matches can seem more concrete than records that are incomplete, damaged, or silent.

That sense of clarity is understandable. Genetic evidence is powerful. But it is not self-explanatory.

DNA does not name places, define relationships on its own, or replace documentary research. It does not explain how or why a connection exists. Instead, it supports conclusions that are already grounded in place, chronology, and association.

This chapter addresses how DNA fits into Irish research, what it can and cannot do, and why treating it as supporting evidence rather than as an answer protects accuracy. Used carefully, DNA strengthens conclusions. Used in isolation, it can create confidence that moves faster than the evidence can support.

Why DNA Feels Definitive

If DNA results felt like a breakthrough, that reaction is understandable. Numbers and charts feel reassuring in ways records often don't. DNA results feel authoritative because they are numerical, scientific, and automated. Match lists arrive pre-ranked. Shared centimorgans suggest precision. Visual tools imply clarity.

That presentation can create the impression that DNA delivers answers directly.

In reality, DNA only shows that two people share genetic material. DNA reflects shared ancestry, not documented relationships (Bettinger, 2016; Thompson, 2013). It does not explain how, when, or through which line without additional context.

Without documentary structure, DNA creates possibility, not conclusion.

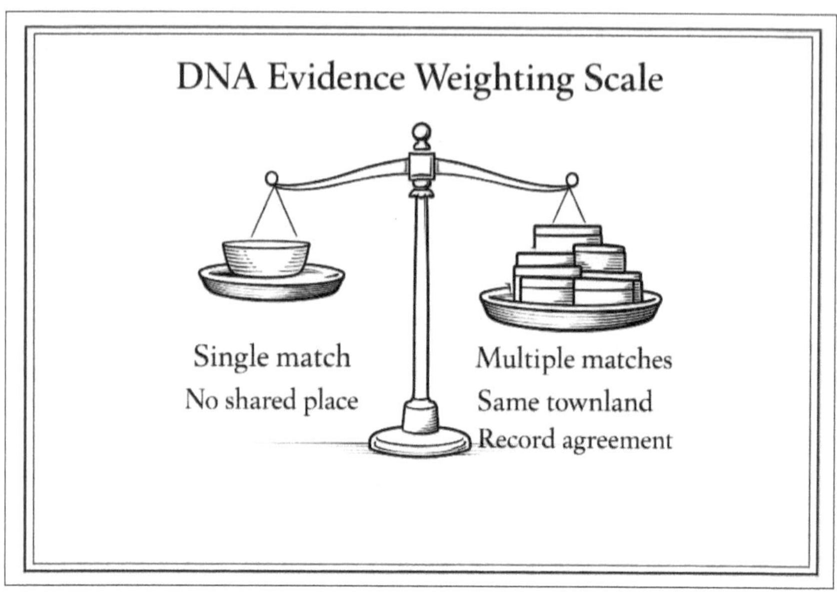

Figure 3. DNA Evidence Weighting Scale

A scale/ladder graphic conveying that DNA evidence becomes more interpretively meaningful when aligned with documentary context, and that multiple moderate matches with shared place/association can outweigh an isolated high match. Likely a graded scale from lower evidentiary weight (DNA alone) to higher (DNA + place + association + records).

What DNA Can Reliably Do

DNA is strongest at confirming that a relationship is possible.

It can support documentary conclusions by showing genetic agreement where one would be expected. It can help rule out relationships that are genetically incompatible. It can identify shared ancestry when paper records are incomplete or missing.

DNA works best when it reinforces a working assumption built from records, place, and association. Recent genetic case studies reinforce this interpretive limit. In a detailed Y-DNA analysis published in Genealogy, Stead (2025) demonstrates how genetic data can strengthen or eliminate proposed lineages only when evaluated against documentary context and clearly framed hypotheses. The study shows that DNA does not resolve identity on its own; it functions as a testing mechanism that can support, refine, or rule out conclusions suggested by records. Used this way, genetic evidence disciplines interpretation rather than replacing it-confirming that DNA is most reliable when constrained by method rather than treated as an answer-generating system.

The pace of change in genetic genealogy makes interpretive discipline more important, not less. A 2025 review of developments in DNA analysis and AI-assisted genealogy notes that while tools increasingly surface connections quickly, they also increase the risk of premature conclusions when results are detached from documentary context (DNA Painter, 2025). Contemporary genetic genealogists continue to stress that shared DNA signals ancestry rather than documented relationship, and that population structure and endogamy complicate interpretation (Erlich et al., 2018). In this environment, DNA strengthens conclusions only when constrained by method rather than treated as an answer-generating system. On its own, it cannot identify which Patrick Reilly in a parish is yours.

Endogamy and Inflated Signals

Irish populations often show endogamy, repeated intermarriage within a limited geographic area over generations.

Endogamy inflates genetic signals and increases the number of matches who appear more closely related than they actually are, requiring slower interpretation (Carmi et al., 2014; ISOGG, n.d.).

Without accounting for endogamy, researchers can overestimate relationship strength, misidentify lines, and collapse multiple ancestral paths into one.

In endogamous contexts, agreement across multiple lines matters more than raw centimorgan totals.

Why Trees Still Matter

DNA does not replace trees. It depends on them.

Interpreting matches requires documented family structures to explain how genetic material could be shared. Trees provide the framework DNA needs to be meaningful.

Trees that treat hypotheses as fact, however, distort DNA interpretation. Errors propagate quickly when trees are copied without scrutiny.

Accurate DNA interpretation depends on accurate, clearly labeled trees.

Using DNA to Test, Not Declare

The most responsible use of DNA is testing hypotheses, not declaring conclusions.

If a paper trail suggests a connection, DNA can be used to look for supporting agreement among descendants of related families from the same area.

If DNA contradicts a working assumption, the working assumption must be reevaluated. DNA is not an override switch. It is one line of evidence among many.

What This Looks Like in Practice

A researcher believes that an immigrant came from a specific townland based on land records and association patterns.

DNA matches include several individuals whose documented ancestry traces to that same area. No strong matches appear from unrelated regions.

This agreement supports the possible connection without proving it. The conclusion remains tentative but stronger.

If DNA had pointed elsewhere, the tentative idea would need revision.

How This Chapter Fits Into Your Research

If you've ever found yourself wondering how DNA supports Irish research without replacing structure, why endogamy complicates interpretation, and how to integrate genetic evidence responsibly.

This book isn't trying to say that DNA will solve brick walls on its own. It shows how DNA strengthens conclusions that are already sound.

If You Remember One Thing

DNA supports conclusions built from records and structure; it does not create them on its own.

Chapter 16: Cross-checking from different angles

Strong genealogical conclusions rarely come from a single record. They come from agreement across multiple, independent sources.

In Irish genealogy, this is not optional. Because direct proof is uncommon, confidence has to be built differently. Cross-checking from different angles provides that structure.

If you've ever found yourself wondering how these three concepts work together, why agreement matters more than volume, and how triangulation protects against overconfidence when certainty is unavailable.

Why Single Records Are Rarely Enough

Most Irish records were created for limited, immediate purposes. They capture fragments of information, not full narratives.

A baptism names parents but not grandparents. A land record places a person but does not explain relationships. A death record may report origin decades after the fact.

Any one of these can mislead if treated as decisive. Agreement across records is what gives them weight.

Repetition Creates Reliability

When the same information appears repeatedly across independent sources, confidence increases.

Repetition might involve a surname recurring in the same townland, the same associates appearing across different record types, or a consistent geographic range across decades.

Repetition does not require identical wording. It requires consistency in meaning.

When repetition is absent, conclusions should remain tentative.

Agreement Is More Than Matching Details

Agreement does not mean every detail matches perfectly.

Irish records often disagree on age, spelling, or minor chronology. Agreement emerges when records point in the same general direction despite surface differences.

For example, several records may place a family within the same cluster of parishes even if none names an exact townland. That agreement carries more weight than a single precise claim that appears nowhere else.

Disagreements in the records matter when they change the bigger picture- not when they're just the usual quirks or errors.

Triangulation: Independent Lines of Support

Triangulation means testing a conclusion using different types of evidence created for different purposes.

A working theory supported by church records, land records, and association patterns is stronger than one supported by church records alone.

Each source type brings different biases and limitations. When they agree, confidence increases because the agreement is unlikely to be accidental.

Triangulation also helps identify weak spots. If one line of evidence contradicts the others, that tension needs examination rather than explanation away.

Avoiding False Agreement

Not all agreement is meaningful.

Agreement can be false when records depend on one another, when later records copy earlier errors, or when multiple trees repeat the same unsupported assumption.

Independent agreement matters more than quantity.

A dozen online trees repeating the same claim do not strengthen it. One independent land record that aligns with church and civil evidence often does.

Knowing which sources are independent is essential.

What This Looks Like in Practice

A researcher proposes that an immigrant came from a specific parish.

Church records in Ireland show a family with the correct name and timeline. Land records place that family in the same townland across decades. In New York, sponsors and neighbors trace back to the same area.

No single record proves the connection. Together, they work toward a conclusion from different angles.

If one element were missing, confidence would drop. If one contradicted the others, the working theory would need revision.

How This Chapter Fits into Your Research

This chapter explains how repetition builds reliability, how agreement strengthens interpretation, and how triangulation protects against stretching the evidence.

It does not promise certainty. It shows how to build conclusions that are proportional, transparent, and defensible.

If You Remember One Thing

Strong conclusions come from independent agreement across multiple sources, not from any single record.

Chapter 17: Endogamy and the Discipline of Slowing Down

Endogamy complicates Irish genealogy in ways that are easy to underestimate. In populations where people married within the same geographic and social circles over generations, genetic signals overlap and intensify.

When this happens, results can feel both convincing and confusing at the same time. Matches multiply. Confidence rises. Clarity does not always follow.

This does not make DNA useless. It changes what careful interpretation requires.

In endogamous contexts, slowing down is not hesitation. It is discipline. Interpreting overlapping genetic and documentary signals takes time, restraint, and proportionate conclusions.

This chapter explains how endogamy affects Irish research, why it can inflate confidence without increasing clarity, and how deliberate slowing protects conclusions when genetic and documentary signals blur together.

What Endogamy Looks Like in Practice

Endogamy occurs when people repeatedly marry within a limited population over time. In Irish contexts, this often reflects geography, landholding patterns, religion, and economic constraint rather than intentional isolation.

Over generations, endogamy creates dense networks of shared ancestry. Individuals may be related through multiple lines at once, even when those relationships are distant or undocumented.

In DNA results, this appears as an unusually high number of matches, inflated shared centimorgan totals, and difficulty separating one ancestral line from another.

Why Endogamy Inflates Confidence

Endogamy can make weak hypotheses feel strong.

When many matches appear to support a conclusion, confidence rises. But in endogamous populations, agreement can reflect shared background rather than a specific relationship.

Multiple matches pointing to the same region may be expected rather than diagnostic. Large shared DNA segments may not indicate recent common ancestry.

Without careful context, endogamy turns volume into false certainty.

Slowing Down as a Method

Endogamy requires a different research posture.

Instead of moving quickly toward conclusions, researchers need to slow down, document assumptions carefully, and resist merging lines prematurely. This is not hesitation. It is discipline.

Slowing down allows patterns to emerge across multiple generations and record types. It creates space to test hypotheses against independent evidence rather than reinforcing them through repetition.

In endogamous contexts, fewer conclusions made carefully are more reliable than many conclusions made quickly.

Adjusting Expectations for DNA

DNA remains valuable in endogamous populations, but expectations must change.

Rather than asking whether a match proves a relationship, it is more useful to ask whether a match is consistent with a proposed structure. Agreement across multiple descendants of the same line matters more than individual match strength.

Segment triangulation, shared match clustering, and geographic context become more important than raw centimorgan numbers.

DNA supports structure. It does not define it.

Protecting Against Premature Merging

One of the most common endogamy-related problems is premature merging.

When genetic signals overlap, it becomes tempting to collapse multiple possible ancestors into one. That shortcut creates long-term instability.

Keeping lines separate longer than feels necessary preserves alternatives and allows evidence to clarify relationships over time. Merging should be the last step, not the first.

What This Looks Like in Practice

A researcher working in a rural Irish parish finds dozens of DNA matches connected to the same area. Many share moderate centimorgan totals.

Instead of merging all lines into a single ancestral couple, the researcher keeps families separate, documents multiple possible connections, and looks for agreement across descendants of specific townlands and households.

Over time, some lines converge while others diverge. Conclusions emerge slowly but hold.

How This Chapter Fits Into Your Research

If you've ever found yourself wondering why endogamy complicates genetic interpretation, why slowing down is a way to keep from jumping to conclusions, and how restraint protects accuracy.

It does not suggest abandoning DNA or avoiding conclusions. It argues for pacing conclusions so they reflect structure rather than signal volume.

If You Remember One Thing

In endogamous research environments, slowing down is not caution- it is accuracy.

Chapter 18: Trees as Hypotheses, Not Truth

Family trees feel authoritative. Names are connected. Dates line up. Relationships appear settled. Once information is placed into a tree, it often feels resolved.

In Irish genealogy, that sense of finality is misleading.

A tree isn't a final answer- it's just your current thinking laid out in one place. They represent current understanding, not permanent truth. Treating them otherwise hardens uncertainty into fact and makes later correction difficult.

This chapter explains why trees should be treated as hypotheses, how overconfidence in tree structure makes later interpretation less stable, and how to build trees that remain useful even when certainty is unavailable.

Why Trees Create False Confidence

Trees organize information visually. That organization can imply certainty even when the evidence is thin.

Once a relationship is drawn, it becomes harder to question. Visual connection replaces analytical caution. Gaps disappear behind clean lines.

In Irish research, where conclusions are often tentative, this effect is especially dangerous. Trees can mask uncertainty rather than reveal it.

When a tree presents hypotheses as facts, later evidence feels disruptive instead of informative.

Trees as Workspaces

A more accurate way to think about trees is as workspaces.

They hold possibilities. They organize evidence. They allow relationships to be tested, revised, and sometimes removed.

A well-built tree makes uncertainty visible. It separates confirmed relationships from proposed ones. It preserves alternatives rather than collapsing them prematurely.

This approach keeps the tree flexible and the research honest.

Labeling Matters

The difference between a working theory and a conclusion is not always the evidence. It is often the label.

Words such as possible, likely, working theory, and unproven communicate status clearly. When those labels are missing, readers assume certainty.

Clear labeling protects both the researcher and anyone who encounters the tree later. It invites collaboration rather than correction.

Unlabeled trees spread errors faster than labeled ones because they look finished when they are not.

Separating Documentation from Interpretation

Another common problem arises when documentation and interpretation blur together.

Sources support facts. Interpretation connects them.

When trees fail to distinguish between what a document states and what the researcher infers, readers cannot evaluate the reasoning. Conclusions appear stronger than they are.

Separating documentation from interpretation makes trees more transparent and easier to revise.

Sharing Trees Responsibly

Most Irish genealogy now happens in shared environments. Trees are copied, merged, and reused.

When trees present hypotheses as facts, errors propagate quickly. Once spread, they are difficult to retract.

Sharing responsibly means labeling uncertainty, avoiding premature merges, and being explicit about the strength of conclusions. It also means accepting revision as part of responsible practice.

A tree that can change is not weak. It is honest.

What This Looks Like in Practice

A researcher proposes that an immigrant belongs to a particular Irish family based on land records, association patterns, and partial DNA agreement.

Instead of merging the family fully, the researcher builds the connection as a working theory, labels it clearly, and documents the reasoning in notes.

If new evidence contradicts the connection, the working assumption can be revised without dismantling the entire tree.

The tree remains a tool, not a verdict.

How This Chapter Fits into Your Research

This chapter explains why trees should be treated as tentative models, how labeling protects accuracy, and how transparency supports collaboration.

It does not argue against building trees. It argues for building them in ways that reflect the limits of the evidence.

Practitioner's Sidebar: Respecting the Shared Tree (Simple Ways to Label Uncertainty Online)

Most Irish research now happens in shared environments-trees get copied, merged, and reused. If uncertainty isn't labeled where people can see it, guesses begin to travel as facts. The goal is not to avoid hypotheses. The goal is to make their status visible.

- Use a visible status label. If your platform supports tags, apply a consistent tag such as Unverified or Working hypothesis to any profile that rests on indirect structure rather than a direct identity statement.

- Add a lead note that follows CLEAR. At the top of the profile, write three short lines: the claim, the reasoning, and the limit-what would strengthen it, and what would overturn it.

- Separate "workspace trees" from "public conclusions." It can be responsible to keep a working tree private while you test competing candidates, then publish only the relationships that are anchored and explained.

The records allow careful inference; they do not allow hidden inference. Labeling is how you keep your work both usable and honest-especially when other people will inherit it.

If You Remember One Thing

A tree should reflect what is known, what is proposed, and what remains uncertain- not hide those differences.

Chapter 19: Research With Care- Pain, Privacy, and Consent

Not every discovery is neutral (Association of Professional Genealogists, 2024; National Society of Genetic Counselors, 2017). Genealogical research can intersect with loss, coercion, adoption, and silence (Trouillot, 1995; Royal Irish Academy, 2010). Genealogy is not only an intellectual exercise. It involves real people, living families, and histories that are sometimes painful.

Irish genealogy in particular intersects with famine, poverty, migration, loss, adoption, and long silence. Records can reveal information that families did not expect to surface or may not be ready to confront.

Responsible research requires more than technical accuracy. It requires care.

In this chapter, you'll see why ethical considerations matter in genealogical work, how to balance discovery with respect, and how to share conclusions without causing unnecessary harm.

Why Genealogical Information Can Hurt

Genealogical discoveries can unsettle long-held beliefs.

Unexpected parentage, adoptions, institutionalization, criminal records, or family estrangements can surface through careful research or DNA testing. For some families, these discoveries reopen wounds rather than answer questions.

The fact that information is historically accurate does not mean it is emotionally neutral.

Researchers need to recognize that truth can carry impact beyond its factual content.

Privacy Is Not Only a Legal Concept

Legal privacy protections vary by jurisdiction and time period. Ethical responsibility goes further.

Just because information can be shared does not mean it should be shared widely or without context. Living individuals may be affected by how information is presented, interpreted, or circulated.

In Irish genealogy, where communities are often tightly connected, careless sharing can ripple outward quickly.

Privacy is about minimizing harm, not avoiding truth.

Consent in Shared Research Spaces

DNA testing and collaborative research often involve people who did not consent to every use of their data.

One person's test can reveal information about others who never tested. Shared trees can expose assumptions as facts. Public notes can circulate interpretations far beyond their original audience.

Responsible researchers think carefully about what they share, how they label conclusions, and where they draw boundaries.

Consent is not always explicit. It must often be inferred and respected cautiously.

Balancing Transparency and Restraint

Transparency is a core value in good research. So is restraint.

Being transparent does not require publishing every tentative idea publicly. It means documenting reasoning clearly and honestly, even if some details are kept private or shared selectively.

Restraint allows research to proceed without forcing disclosure before families are ready or conclusions are firm.

Accuracy and kindness are not opposing values. They reinforce each other.

Sharing Difficult Findings

When research uncovers sensitive information, how it is shared matters as much as what is shared.

Context should be provided. Uncertainty should be stated clearly. Language should be neutral rather than sensational.

In many cases, it is appropriate to share findings privately before making them public, or to limit access to sensitive details altogether.

Ethical research considers downstream impact, not just immediate correctness.

How This Chapter Fits Into Your Research

This chapter emphasizes that responsible Irish genealogy combines methodic rigor with ethical awareness.

It does not argue against uncovering difficult truths. It argues for doing so thoughtfully, with attention to privacy, consent, and human consequence.

Care is part of accuracy.

If You Remember One Thing

Good genealogy is not only about what you can prove, but about how you handle what you learn.

Deep Dive: A Conclusion That Can Survive Scrutiny

Unit IV is where many Reilly projects either become strong-or become permanently fragile. DNA results arrive with numbers and charts. Trees fill in visually. It feels like the moment to lock things down. This unit insists on a different outcome: a conclusion that can be shared without apology because its limits are visible. DNA is used the way this manuscript teaches it: as supporting evidence that strengthens a structure already grounded in place, chronology, and association. If a cluster of matches aligns with the same narrowed Irish region you reached through documentary work, confidence rises. If it doesn't, the disagreement is not a crisis-it's information that prevents a wrong merge from hardening into a permanent claim.

This is where CLEAR becomes the finishing discipline. The Reilly conclusion is written as:

- What is known (documented Brooklyn identity and network)

- What is proposed (a specific Irish candidate or local network that best fits the accumulated structure)

What remains uncertain (the missing piece you do not have, and what would change your conclusion)

The records allow a responsible statement: "This is the best-supported working hypothesis given the convergence of evidence, and it remains open to revision." They do not allow: "Case closed."

And because other people will inherit what you publish-through shared trees, copied profiles, and DNA networks-this unit treats clarity as an ethical act, not just a methodological one.

Closing Note

If this book slowed you down, challenged assumptions, or left some questions open, that doesn't mean it failed you. It means you now have a way to keep working without distorting the past or yourself. Irish genealogy rarely ends with certainty. For many lines, it cannot.

That reality is not a failure of research or persistence. It is a reflection of how records were created, what survived, and what they were never meant to preserve. Working responsibly within those limits is not settling for less. It is choosing accuracy over comfort.

Throughout this book, the emphasis has been on method rather than outcome. Clear questions. Proportional conclusions. Honest uncertainty. Respect for both records and people.

These practices do not guarantee answers. They do something more important: They produce work that can be trusted, shared, revised, and built upon without apology.

Good genealogy does not require perfect proof. It requires care- care in how questions are framed, how evidence is weighed, how conclusions are labeled, and how discoveries are handled.

When certainty is unavailable, clarity remains possible. And clarity is enough.

References

Association of Professional Genealogists. (2024). Code of ethics and professional practices. https://www.apgen.org/code_of_ethics.php

Ayeni, O. B., Omigbodun, O. M., & Onibalusi, O. T. (2025). Kinship as Evidence: Genealogy, Law, and the Politics of Recognition. Genealogy, 9(4), 138. https://doi.org/10.3390/genealogy9040138

Bakewell, O., de Haas, H., & Kubal, A. (2012). Migration systems, pioneer migrants and the role of agency. Journal of Critical Realism, 11(4), 413-437.

Bettinger, B. (2016). The family tree guide to DNA testing and genetic genealogy. Family Tree Books.

Bettinger, B. (2019). The Shared cM Project 3.0. The Genetic Genealogist. https://thegeneticgenealogist.com

Bettinger, B., & Wayne, D. (2016). Genetic genealogy in practice. National Genealogical Society.

Bloch, M. (1953). The historian's craft. Alfred A. Knopf.

Board for Certification of Genealogists. (2025). BCG application guide. https://bcgcertification.org

Board for Certification of Genealogists. (2021). Genealogy standards (2nd ed. rev.). Ancestry.

Bodnar, J. (1985). The transplanted: A history of immigrants in urban America. Indiana University Press.

Bommes, M., & Morawska, E. (Eds.). (2005). International migration research: Constructions, omissions, and the promises of interdisciplinarity. Ashgate.

Bourdieu, P. (1977). Outline of a theory of practice. Cambridge University Press.

Braudel, F. (1980). On history. University of Chicago Press.

Brigham Young University, Family History Library. (n.d.). Ireland research outline [PDF]. https://files.lib.byu.edu/family-history-library/research-outlines/Europe/Ireland.pdf

Carmi, S., Hui, K. Y., Kochav, E., Liu, X., Xue, J., Grady, F., & Pe'er, I. (2014). Sequencing an Ashkenazi reference panel supports population-targeted personal genomics and illuminates Jewish and European origins. Nature Communications, 5, 4835. https://doi.org/10.1038/ncomms5835

Cooke, R. (2019). Researching family history in the digital age. Pen & Sword Family History.

Department of Culture, Communications and Sport. (2018, May 25). Catholic parish registers in the National Library. https://www.gov.ie/en/department-of-culture-communications-and-sport/services/catholic-parish-registers-in-the-national-library/

de Haas, H. (2010). The internal dynamics of migration processes: A theoretical inquiry. Journal of Ethnic and Migration Studies, 36(10), 1587-1617. https://doi.org/10.1080/1369183X.2010.489361

Diner, H. R. (1983). Erin's daughters in America: Irish immigrant women in the nineteenth century. Johns Hopkins University Press.

DNA Painter. (2025). Genealogy and DNA: A review of 2025. https://blog.dnapainter.com

Ellis Island Foundation. (n.d.). Passenger records and immigration history. https://www.statueofliberty.org/discover/passenger-ship-search/

Erlich, Y., Shor, T., Pe'er, I., & Carmi, S. (2018). Identity inference of genomic data using long-range familial searches. Science, 362(6415), 690-694. https://doi.org/10.1126/science.aau4832

Fischer, D. H. (1970). Historians' fallacies: Toward a logic of historical thought. Harper & Row.

Gabaccia, D. R. (2000). Italy's many diasporas. UCL Press.

Ginzburg, C. (1989). Clues, myths, and the historical method (J. Tedeschi & A. Tedeschi, Trans.). Johns Hopkins University Press.

Great Britain. Office of the General Valuation of Ireland. (1847-1864). General valuation of rateable property in Ireland. FamilySearch Catalog. https://www.familysearch.org/en/search/catalog/218030

International Society of Genetic Genealogy. (n.d.). ISOGG Wiki. https://isogg.org/wiki/Main_Page

Kennett, D. J. (2019). The surname handbook: A guide to genetic genealogy. The History Press.

Knaflic, S. N. (2015). Storytelling with data: A data visualization guide for business professionals. Wiley.

Kuhn, T. S. (1962). The structure of scientific revolutions. University of Chicago Press.

Massey, D. (1994). Space, place, and gender. University of Minnesota Press.

Massey, D. S., Arango, J., Hugo, G., Kouaouci, A., Pellegrino, A., & Taylor, J. E. (1998). Worlds in motion: Understanding international migration at the end of the millennium. Oxford University Press.

Mills, E. S. (2017). Evidence explained: Citing history sources from artifacts to cyberspace (3rd ed., rev.). Genealogical Publishing Company.

Morawska, E. (2001). Structuring migration: The case of Polish income-seeking travelers to the West. Theory and Society, 30(1), 47-80. https://doi.org/10.1023/A:1011081228016

National Archives and Records Administration. (n.d.). Immigration and naturalization records. https://www.archives.gov/research/immigration

National Archives of Ireland. (n.d.). Guide to what records survive. https://nationalarchives.ie/help-with-research/research-guides/

National Archives of Ireland. (n.d.). Understanding Irish administrative divisions. https://nationalarchives.ie/help-with-research/understanding-irish-records/

National Genealogical Society. (2015). NGS standards for sound genealogical research. https://www.ngsgenealogy.org/genealogy-resources/standards/

National Library of Ireland. (n.d.). Catholic parish registers: Scope and coverage. https://registers.nli.ie/about

National Library of Ireland. (2021). Catholic parish registers geodata: Parish boundaries (GeoJSON dataset). https://data.gov.ie/dataset/catholic-parish-registers-geodata

National Society of Genetic Counselors. (2017). Code of ethics. Journal of Genetic Counseling, 27(1), 6-8. https://doi.org/10.1007/s10897-017-0166-8

New York City Department of Records and Information Services. (n.d.). Historical vital records. https://www.nyc.gov/site/records/historical-records/vital-records.page

New York City Municipal Archives. (n.d.). Historical vital records of NYC (NYC Historical Vital Records Project). https://a860-historicalvitalrecords.nyc.gov/

New York State Archives. (n.d.). Birth, marriage, and death records. https://www.archives.nysed.gov/research/birth-marriage-death-records

New York State Archives. (n.d.). Genealogy. https://www.archives.nysed.gov/research/genealogy

Ó Gráda, C. (1994). Ireland: A new economic history, 1780-1939. Oxford University Press.

Peirce, C. S. (1931-1958). Collected papers of Charles Sanders Peirce (C. Hartshorne & P. Weiss, Eds., Vols. 1-6; A. W. Burks, Ed., Vols. 7-8). Harvard University Press.

Perl, J. (2025, December 30). Genealogy and DNA: A review of 2025. DNA Painter Blog. https://blog.dnapainter.com/blog/genealogy-and-dna-a-review-of-2025/

Placenames Database of Ireland. (n.d.). Place categories and townlands. https://www.logainm.ie/en/about/place-categories

Ralph, P., & Coop, G. (2013). The geography of recent genetic ancestry across Europe. PLoS Biology, 11(5), e1001555. https://doi.org/10.1371/journal.pbio.1001555

Royal Irish Academy. (2010). Ensuring integrity in Irish research: A discussion document. Royal Irish Academy. https://www.interacademies.org/publication/ensuring-integrity-irish-research

Shan, F., & Luther, K. (2024). Reexamining technological support for genealogy research, collaboration, and education. arXiv. https://arxiv.org/abs/2411.07869Society of American Archivists. (2020). SAA core values statement and code of ethics. https://www2.archivists.org/statements/saa-core-values-statement-and-code-of-ethics

Stead, P., Haddrill, P. R., & Macdonald, A. F. (2025). What Can Y-DNA Analysis Reveal About the Scottish Hay Noble Lineage? Genealogy, 9(4), 132. https://doi.org/10.3390/genealogy9040132

Thompson, E. A. (2013). Identity by descent. Cambridge University Press. https://doi.org/10.1017/CBO9781139083977

Thompson, E. P. (1963). The making of the English working class. Vintage.

Trouillot, M.-R. (1995). Silencing the past: Power and the production of history. Beacon Press.

Ulrich, L. T. (1990). A midwife's tale. Knopf.

U.S. Bureau of the Census. (n.d.). History of the U.S. census. https://www.census.gov/history/www/through_the_decades/overview/

Wright, S. (1969). Evolution and the genetics of populations (Vol. 2: The theory of gene frequencies). University of Chicago Press.

Yakel, E. (2004). Seeking information, seeking connections, seeking meaning: Genealogy and family history. Information Research, 10(1). http://informationr.net/ir/10-1/paper205.html

Acknowledgement

This book emerged from years of shared work with the Cavan Cousins research group. Through collaborative problem-solving, careful disagreement, and sustained attention to what the records could and could not support, that community shaped how I learned to think about Irish genealogy as a disciplined method rather than a search for certainty.

I am grateful to the many researchers who contributed questions, challenged assumptions, documented uncertainty honestly, and prioritized clarity over closure. The strengths of this book reflect what I learned through that shared work; responsibility for its interpretations and conclusions remains my own.

About The Author

Laura Woodward

Laura Woodward is a founder and organizer of the Cavan Cousins Project. She holds a Ph.D. in social psychology, which informs her interest in how people make meaning from incomplete evidence.

The Cavan Cousins Project is a collaborative community. It connects descendants of Irish families through documentary research, shared DNA evidence, and shared family trees.

Her interest is in Irish genealogy and the Irish diaspora, with particular attention to migration from Ireland to New York, Canada and Australia. Her rule of thumb is, clarity matters more than certainty, and careful method is a form of respect.

Glossary

Absence (as Evidence)
A documented lack of a record that, when searched thoroughly and within known record coverage, can narrow possibilities or rule out assumptions without proving a specific conclusion.

Anchor (Evidence Anchor)
A stable point of reference, often a land record, repeated location, or long-term association that fixes an individual in time and place without asserting identity or relationship.

Association
A recurring connection between individuals shown through proximity, shared records, sponsors, witnesses, neighbors, or community participation rather than explicit statements of relationship.

Boundary Behavior
Patterns created when people live near overlapping civil, religious, or administrative jurisdictions, causing records for the same family to appear in different parishes or systems.

Cluster (Settlement or Migration Cluster)
A group of individuals who appear together repeatedly in records due to shared migration paths, settlement patterns, or community ties, used to narrow research questions rather than prove identity.

Consistency (of Method)
The disciplined application of the same research standards, thresholds, terminology, and documentation practices across time and family lines to protect accuracy and transparency.

Continuity
Repeated appearance of a person or family in the same place, with the same associates, across multiple records and over time, used as a stronger identifier than name alone.

Evidence-Based Working Assumption
A clearly labeled, tentative conclusion grounded in available evidence, used to guide further research while remaining explicitly open to revision.

Hidden Assumptions
Unexamined beliefs, such as name uniqueness, complete record survival, or fixed boundaries that shape research questions and interpretation without being stated or tested.

Hypothesis (Genealogical)
A structured explanation for observed patterns in the evidence that invites testing and revision, distinct from guessing or asserting unproven claims as fact.

Identity (Emergent)
A conclusion about who a person was that develops gradually through accumulated evidence, continuity, and constraint, rather than being established by a single record.

Jurisdiction Stack
A layered description of the overlapping administrative, civil, and religious systems that may apply to a single place, used to interpret records accurately.

Negative Search
A documented search that produced no relevant result, recorded in sufficient detail so that its absence can inform interpretation rather than be repeated or forgotten.

Overinterpretation
Assigning stronger meaning or certainty to evidence than the record can reasonably support, often by treating context, association, or absence as proof.

Place-First Research
An approach that prioritizes geographic stability, townland, parish, and walkable area before attempting to assign identity or family relationships.

Premature Merging
Combining records or individuals based on name similarity or partial overlap before sufficient evidence supports shared identity, often leading to compounded error.

Proportional Conclusion
A conclusion stated only as strongly as the evidence allows, with its limits
clearly visible and uncertainty explicitly acknowledged.

Record-Limited Environment
A research context in which records are incomplete, unevenly surviving, or not
designed to answer modern genealogical questions, requiring restraint and
method rather than certainty.

Scale (of a Research Question)
The size and ambition of a question relative to what the surviving records can
realistically answer; oversized questions stall research, while properly scaled ones
allow progress.

Sideways Reading
An interpretive method that focuses on neighbors, sponsors, witnesses, and
recurring associates to build context and structure when direct lineage evidence
is missing.

Structure (in Research)
An organized framework of place, time, association, and documentation that
allows identity to emerge gradually without forcing conclusions.

Tentative Conclusion
A labeled outcome that reflects current evidence while remaining open to
challenge, correction, or refinement as new information appears.

Transparency (in Method)
Clear documentation of reasoning, uncertainty, assumptions, and limitations so
others can evaluate, replicate, or revise the work responsibly.

Walkable Set
The group of neighboring townlands or parishes realistically accessible based
on terrain, roads, and lived geography rather than modern map distance.

www.ingramcontent.com/pod-product-compliance
Lightning Source LLC
Chambersburg PA
CBHW051457130726
47987CB00005B/2363